The Complete Book of ROCK TUMBLING

The Complete Book

Christopher S. Hyde & Richard A. Matthews

of **ROCK TUMBLING**

Chilton Book Company · *Radnor, Pennsylvania*

Copyright © 1977 by Christopher S. Hyde and Richard A. Matthews
First Edition   All Rights Reserved
Published in Radnor, Pa., by Chilton Book Company and simultaneously
in Don Mills, Ontario, Canada, by Thomas Nelson & Sons, Ltd.
Library of Congress Catalog Card No. 77-70331
ISBN: 0-8019-6236-6 *hardcover*
ISBN: 0-8019-6237-4 *paperback*
Manufactured in the United States of America

1 2 3 4 5 6 7 8 9 0   6 5 4 3 2 1 0 9 8 7

Contents

Acknowledgments, ix
List of Illustrations, xi
List of Tables, xiii

Chapter 1
Introduction   1
    Ancient Abrading and Carving Techniques, 2
    The First Mechanical Tumbler, 3
    Lapidary as a Hobby, 4

Chapter 2
Locating and Choosing Tumbling Materials   7
    Gem-Hunting Guides, 8
    Mineralogical Societies, 9
    Rock Shops and Rockhounds, 9
    Prospecting, 9

Chapter 3
Selecting and Preparing Tumbling Materials   14
    Hardness (Mohs Scale), 14
    Type of Fracture, 15
    Grain and Pitting, 16
    Color and Inclusions, 17
    Cleanliness, 18
    Characteristics of Purchased Materials, 20
    Selecting Quality Beach Pebbles, 21

Chapter 4
Equipment and Workshop Requirements   22
    Small Tumblers, 22
    Medium-Sized Tumblers, 26
    Large Tumblers, 30
    Setting up a Workshop, 30
    Supplies, 32

Chapter 5
Building Your Own Rotary Tumbler   35
    Construction Supplies, 35
    Tumbler Design: Sample Calculations, 39

Chapter 6
Vibrating Tumblers   46
    Types, 46
    Advantages and Disadvantages, 49
    Charging a Vibrating Model, 50
    Tumbling Time, 51
    A Test, 54

Chapter 7
Getting Started—Rough Grind   57
    Breaking Rough, 57
    Determining Tumbling Loads, 59
    Charging the Tumbler, 62
    Rough Grind, 66
    Second Rough Grind, 69

Chapter 8
Intermediate Grind, Prepolish and Polish   72
    Intermediate Grind, 72
    Prepolish Tumbling, 76
    Polish Cycle, 83
    Burnishing, 87

Chapter 9
What's Going On in There?   90
    Effects of Barrel Shape, 90
    Tumbling Speeds, 90
    Weight and Solution Viscosity, 92
    Chemical Action, 93
    Bacterial Action, 94

Chapter 10
Tumbling Slabs and Preforms   95
    Preparation of Preforms, 95
    Tumbling Small Slabs, 96
    Tumbling Large Slabs, 99
    Preparing Saw Ends, 101

Contents　　　　　　　　　　　　　　　　　　　　　　　　　　　　　vii

Chapter 11
What Went Wrong?　　　　　　　　　　　　　　　　　　　　　　　　　104
　　　　　Common Defects and Corrective Measures, 104
　　　　　Treating Imperfect Stones, 109

Chapter 12
Setting Baroque Stones　　　　　　　　　　　　　　　　　　　　　　112
　　　　　Adhesives, 112
　　　　　Techniques, 114
　　　　　Selecting and Using Jewelry Findings, 117
　　　　　Lucite Embedding, 129

Chapter 13
Handmade Baroque Settings　　　　　　　　　　　　　　　　　　　131
　　　　　Wire Wrapping, 131
　　　　　Sheet Metal Settings, 138
　　　　　Built-Up Settings, 141

Chapter 14
Other Tumbler Uses and Auxiliary Equipment　　　　　　　　　　149
　　　　　Burnishing Finished Jewelry, 149
　　　　　Tumbling Other Materials, 153
　　　　　Diamond Saws, 153
　　　　　Slabbing Small Stones, 157
　　　　　Notching and Grooving, 158
　　　　　Cutting Preforms, 160
　　　　　Grinding Wheels, 160
　　　　　Drilling Holes, 162

Appendix　　　　　　　　　　　　　　　　　　　　　　　　　　　　　167
　　　　　Commonly Tumbled Stones: Characteristics
　　　　　　and Folklore, 167
　　　　　Glossary, 173
　　　　　Sources of Supply, 177

Index　　　　　　　　　　　　　　　　　　　　　　　　　　　　　　179

Acknowledgments

The authors are grateful to the following firms and individuals who supplied valuable information and photographs for this book: Calway Inc.; Capri Products, Inc.; Covington Engineering Corp.; The Exolon Company; Ferrara Industries; Geode Industries, Inc.; Hughes Associates; Lortone Inc.; A. D. McBurney; M-Line Manufacturing Company; the Norton Company; Star Diamond Industries; Swest Inc.; Viking Equipment Division of Geode Industries; Helen Drutt Galleries; Sid Meyers Clearly Stoned, Inc.; Photo Associates of Philadelphia and Dick Rothman.

List of Illustrations

Figure		
1-1	Tumbled beach pebbles	2
1-2	Tumbled stones and slabs	5
2-1	Rock hunting in quarries	8
2-2	Exposed rock strata	10
2-3	Rock collecting	11
2-4	Avoid fractured walls	12
3-1	Conchoidal fracturing in goldstone	15
3-2	Fractured stone surface	16
3-3	Base material	18
3-4	Disposing of porous rough	19
4-1	Small tumblers with rubber barrels	23
4-2	Another tumbler	24
4-3	Two-barrel tumblers	25
4-4	Triple-barrel tumbler	26
4-5	Hexagonal barrel	27
4-6	Single-shaft tumbler	28
4-7	Medium-sized tumbler	28
4-8	Single-shaft tumbler	29
4-9	Tumbling units	29
4-10	Prepackaged kits	33
4-11	Materials for processing	34
5-1	Mechanical layout for tumbler	37
5-2	Construction of stops	38
5-3	Placement of stops	39
6-1	Vibrasonic unit	47
6-2	Vibratory tumbler	47
6-3	Adjusting tumbler vibration	48
6-4	Small vibratory tumblers	50
6-5	Charging the barrel	53

Figure		
6-6	Spalling in obsidian	55
7-1	Breaking up rough	58
7-2	Breaking stone that fractures conchoidally	58
7-3	Balanced and even loads	59
7-4	Examination of rough	60
7-5	Obsidian samples	61
7-6	Proper water level	67
7-7	Rough ground stone ready for next stage	68
7-8	Inspection between stages	69
7-9	Sequence of breaking and sorting steps	70
7-10	Internal fracturing in carnelian	71
8-1	Photo series: steps between each tumbling stage	74–75
8-2	Internal fracturing in amethyst	76
8-3	Labeling tumbler barrel	77
8-4	Apache Tears, perfectly finished	80
8-5	Level of stones	81
8-6	Completed intermediate stage	82
8-7	Panning out pellet medium	82
8-8	Test polishing on buffing wheel	86
8-9	Buffing determines if prepolish is complete	86
9-1	Theoretical model of striated layers inside tumbler	91
9-2	Slurry consistency	93
10-1	Tumbled preforms	96

List of Illustrations

Figure

10-2	Tumble-ready slabs	97
10-3	Tumbled-polished slabs	98
10-4	Slab clock face and attachment of motor	99
10-5	Vibratory slab tumbling	100
10-6	Slab racks	101
10-7	Preparing saw ends	101
10-8	Tumble-ready saw ends	102
10-9	Preformed shapes	103
11-1	Carry-over of abrasives	105
11-2	Pitting in carnelians	107
11-3	Internal fracturing vs. surface blistering	108
11-4	Repaired fractures in slab	110
11-5	Perfect polish on Apache Tears	111
12-1	Epoxies for setting stones	113
12-2	Two-part adhesives	113
12-3	Mounted stones are cured	115
12-4	Convenient setting tool	116
12-5	Methylene chloride removes cured epoxy	116
12-6	Samples of commercial settings	117
12-7	Opening and closing a jump ring	119
12-8	Baroque stones in settings	120
12-9	Sterling silver jewelry settings	121
12-10	Mounted, tumbled garnets	122
12-11	Constructing a stone-sorting screen	123
12-12	Necklace of wrapped baroques	124
12-13	Stone clustering technique	124
12-14	Filigree cross with stone clusters	125
12-15	Eye agate pendant	126
12-16	Gem trees	128
12-17	Display stands	129
12-18	Semiprecious stones embedded in Lucite	130
13-1	Basic tools for stone setting	132

Figure

13-2	Pendant and earring set	133
13-3	Cross sections of silver wire	134
13-4	Setting stones in wire forms	135
13-5	Moebius strip	136
13-6	Agate pendant set in braided silver	137
13-7	Silver stone cages	138
13-8	Sheet metal settings	139
13-9	Botswana agate in sheet metal setting	140
13-10	Cutting prongs	140
13-11	Agate set in triangle of sterling	141
13-12	Photo series: soldering a silver stone setting	142
13-13	Prong setting	143
13-14	Brazilian agate pendant	144
13-15	Picket bezel setting	145
13-16	Ring with multiple-prong setting	146
13-17	Herkimer diamond in cage variation	147
13-18	Electroformed jewelry: toque, brooch and neckpiece	147
14-1	Tumbling shot	150
14-2	Charged tumbler	151
14-3	Silver shapes before and after tumbling	152
14-4	Three models of diamond trim saw	154
14-5	Swing arm diamond slab saw	155
14-6	Photo series: formation of cement block to cut small slabs	156–157
14-7	Notching a baroque	159
14-8	Agate grooved with diamond saw	159
14-9	Lapidary grinder-polishers	161
14-10	Setting stones for drilling	163
14-11	Ring with interchangeable stone	164
14-12	Drilling equipment	165
14-13	Drilling a slab	165

List of Color Illustrations

Figure

1. Tumble-polished stones and slabs
2. Red hematite polish on amazonite
3. Ring designs using wrapped stones
4. Slab used as a clock face
5. Botswana agate slab in silver setting
6. Pendants of garnet, sapphire, diamond and emerald set in Lucite
7. Brooch of electroformed gold on silver

Figure

8. Choker of agate slab and amethyst crystals
9. Agate pendant with braided silver wire
10. Moss agate in sheet metal setting
11. Clean piece of tiger-eye rough
12. Fractured surface of Brazilian agate

List of Tables

Table
1. Tumbler Operating Speeds as a Function of Effective Barrel Diameter, 40
2. Suggested Shaft Diameters, 45
3. Compatible Tumbling Materials by Group, 63
4. Coarse Grind in 60/90 Wire-Saw Abrasive or 80 Mesh, 64
5. Intermediate or Fine Grind, 78
6. Prepolish, 84
7. Polish, 88

The Complete Book of ROCK TUMBLING

Chapter 1

Introduction

The first rock tumbler was the ocean. As anyone who has been to the beach can testify, it continues to polish all kinds of material. Beginning with the sharp-edged fragments of undersea boulders or pieces eaten away from the shore, it moves them up and down the beach with each successive wave, wearing away the edges and corners through abrasion against sand and other stones. Except when the waves are high, most of the grinding takes place as the stone *slides* against its neighbors—just as it does in a man-made tumbler. It is usually only the smaller pebble that tumbles end over end, so that most of the largest stones found on the beach have two relatively flat sides and rounded edges. The sea's rough material also makes a difference: in an area where the rock is predominantly quartz, the pebbles will be more rounded overall than in a spot where shale or feldspar breaks into slabs along cleavage planes. The egg-like Cape May diamonds of the New Jersey coast are quartz pebbles, often individual crystals, that have been rounded by wave action. They become water-clear again when the frosted surface is removed by further tumbling with finer abrasives.

The sea with its coarse abrasives gives such pebbles a "rough grind." The stone is rounded and irregularities are smoothed out, but the surface seems polished only while it remains wet, as anyone knows who has carried home a beach pebble and let it dry.

Fig. 1-1 Tumbled beach pebbles often have pleasant shapes.

ANCIENT ABRADING AND CARVING TECHNIQUES

Ever since men began to carry pretty stones around as amulets or for personal adornment, they have longed for some way to keep the wet sheen that seemed so attractive. It was probably the Chinese, about 4,500 B.C., who found a way to take the natural process of abrasion a step further, still using water and sand. Their perfect spheres of rock crystal were made by chipping the quartz until it formed a rough ball, then rolling the ball up and down a trough filled with water and sand until it was smooth. Progressively finer sand was used as the work advanced, sometimes over a period of years, the last polish being given with a rouge of some finely ground stone (perhaps ground garnet) to eliminate all scratches and provide a perfectly clear surface.

Fine carving of crystal and jade was also done with sand, sometimes with crushed sapphires or garnets, by means of a bow drill. The drill point, a hollow reed, was rotated on the surface in a slurry of powdered abrasive and water. For exceedingly fine work, a single point of sapphire was used.

The Chinese are also thought to have been the inventors of the very ingredient that makes modern rock tumbling practical: silicon carbide abrasive. Ordinary sand wears out as an abrasive fairly rapidly. Individuals grains lose their sharpness and cutting edges, or they become pulverized into a powder too fine to have much cutting action. The Chinese

Introduction

crystal and jade polishers discovered that sand on which a fire had been built kept its abrasive qualities much longer than ordinary sand. They were soon firing sand and charcoal in kilns to obtain larger quantities of the new abrasive, a form of silicon carbide. Most of the sharp, long-lasting grits used in rock tumbling today are variants of this ancient material only recently rediscovered (in 1891).

THE FIRST MECHANICAL TUMBLER

None of the ancient stone carving or polishing techniques, whether used for Chinese jade, Egyptian jasper or Aztec crystal, can be considered a form of tumbling, although all of them involved grinding the stone with progressively finer abrasives in a water solution. Ancient civilizations, except perhaps for Atlantis, seem to have lacked the constant, *uniform*, mechanical power source that makes tumbling practical.

Primitive techniques do, however, have one thing in common with tumbling, as opposed to other methods of gem cutting. They retain as much as possible of the precious material, keeping the natural contours of the original stone.

Oriental gem cutters still polish the entire stone, merely highlighting the most colorful areas, instead of cutting these out and discarding the rest. Medieval jewelers, before faceting was invented, did the same thing. They preferred not to waste any of the stone which, in addition to being extremely costly, was believed to possess magical virtues—amethyst prevented drunkenness, turquoise warded off injury from falls, bloodstone neutralized poison, and so on. (Since the tumbling method also retains these virtues, we have listed some of them in the Appendix.) The results of this type of gem cutting were large, somewhat irregularly shaped stones that can be seen in museums on breastplates, crowns, ceremonial armor and religious vestments. Such stones, usually flattened on one side so that they could be mounted in bezels, are known as baroque-cut gems. Medieval baroques included emeralds, rubies, sapphires and even diamonds which were ground using another diamond or diamond dust. Tumbled stones are still called baroques because of their naturally irregular shapes.

The rock tumbler used by today's hobbyist is a relatively modern invention, requiring, as it does, a constant driving power—electricity—uniform, long-lasting abrasives—silicon carbides—and a water-tight, abrasion-resistant container.

No one knows for sure who first used a tumbler for rock polishing. The principle of tumbling has been used in industry for many years to grind, polish and remove burrs from masses of small parts, a process which would be too costly and time consuming if each part were finished individually. Time in the tumbler, amount and type of abrasive and type of tumbling action are carefully controlled so that the process provides exactly the degree of finish required without weakening or damaging the part itself. Even rubber and plastic parts are tumbled to remove flash remaining from the molding step. Liquid nitrogen at −320°F (−195.5°C) chills the tumbler so that the flash becomes brittle and breaks off as the parts collide in the tumbling drum.

The first rock tumblers did not even approach industrial sophistication. They were machines put together by agate collectors in the West and the Midwest to clean and rough grind their finds. Often the tumbler served only to provide a clean surface, making inspection easier before the stones were cut and polished by some other method.

The typical early tumbler consisted of a barrel made from a paint can or some other convenient container, riding on two lengths of pipe—one of which was fitted with a pulley—driven by an electric motor. The speed of tumbler rotation was controlled by varying the size of the pulley. All degrees of sophistication except for rubber lining could be and were built into these early machines, but the basic principle remained a constantly rotating can, about half full of stones, water, abrasive and assorted exotic ingredients. The main improvement since then has been the rubber liner that provides long wear and better tumbling action.

Tumbling was an esoteric art. Old-timers who somehow achieved consistently good polishes on their stones had carefully guarded recipes, including the amount and type of abrasive, the time in each polishing step, the speed of the tumbler and a glorious assortment of glop from crushed walnut husks and sugar to corncobs and chopped banana peels.

In time, the practice was reduced to a more scientific level as abrasives and additives were manufactured specifically for use in a growing hobby. Compact, inexpensive tumblers were marketed nationwide in a variety of sizes and shapes as interest in rock polishing increased. Swishing and rumbling could be heard in American basements from coast to coast.

LAPIDARY AS A HOBBY

Unfortunately, the benefits of scientific know-how were reaped mainly by professionals, craftsmen who manufacture polished stone jewelry, or large manufacturers in the United States and Mexico who tumble polish tons of semiprecious stones each day. The part-time hobbyist, until now, has been left with a coffee can on a pipe rack and an assortment of tumbling instructions, some of which work some of the time on some types of stones.

Lack of information has produced a great deal of disappointment: a majority of the tumblers purchased wind up in the attic after one or two uses. This is a waste, and not only of an investment in time and money, *because the amateur using inexpensive standard equipment can produce better gemstones than the professional.*

Fig. 1-2 Typical tumble-polished stones and slabs, including mounted stones.

Once he has learned the mechanics of tumble polishing, the hobbyist often has more time than the pro to spend upon decisions that make the difference between average and superior gemstones—selection and grading of rough material, sorting between grinds and determining the degree of final polish. The professional lapidary, with deadlines to meet and hired help working to set time schedules, must compromise. He produces a saleable gemstone. The hobbyist who is working because of interest in the craft should not settle for anything less than a perfect stone.

In Chapters 4 through 6 we will discuss the pros and cons of some of the more popular types of tumblers available today. Any one of these, provided the workmanship is reasonably good, will produce excellent results. The problem that has relegated so many to the attic is, we believe, twofold: a lack of explicit instructions—in spite of the instruction booklets that come with most units, many important aspects of the craft are left to chance; and impatience. Impatience is responsible for most bad work, but nowhere is this more true than in lapidary. With the prevalence of saleable "good enough" stones, most people have never seen a really perfect tumble-polished stone. The rough work that tourists bring home from Mexico or South America is to a good baroque as a piece of glass is to a diamond.

This book is designed to take the beginner or the more advanced amateur step-by-step through the tumbling process from beginning to end, then to show some of the many attractive uses for baroque gems. Alterations in technique required for certain types of stones are listed, by variety of materials, in Tables 4–7. Instructions are as highly detailed and explicit as we can make them. If they are followed, any well-made tumbling machine will produce better gemstones than any seen on the market. If it does not, you are doing something wrong and should turn to Chapter 11, *What Went Wrong?*, find a description of the defect, learn what to do to correct it, and begin again. If correct procedures are adhered to, you can be as confident of a perfect gemstone as of the fact that pure water solidifies at sea level at a temperature of 32°F (0°C). Both expectations are based on the same knowledge of physical theory.

Although there is no magic involved in rock tumbling, it does require time, close attention to detail, cleanliness and a certain amount of craftsmanship. But isn't that what a hobby is all about? And rock tumbling has this to recommend it—you can seldom ruin a good stone completely, in the same way you can ruin a piece of mahogany or a ceramic jug. You may lose some time through error, and your stone may be a little smaller when it's finished, but it will still be a gem.

Chapter 2

Locating and Choosing Tumbling Materials

Tumbling materials can be found almost anywhere. Every state has at least a few locations where you can find polishable stones. The question you will have to ask yourself is: "What is my time worth?" If tumbling is an adjunct to a rock collecting hobby or you enjoy a day's treasure hunting, by all means look for your own materials. This will give you the extra satisfaction of having carried through all the steps yourself. But if you want to polish stones for jewelry, or if you find yourself without an abundance of free time (and luck), you will be much better off buying rough materials.

When prospecting, you will spend at least a full day locating the site and mining the stones you want, and you will probably bring home a few pounds at most. You can buy better materials for a fraction of the cost, even if you value your time at less than the minimum wage. Rock hunting is like fishing, though. Hardly anyone is going to calculate the extra cost and go to the fish market instead of getting out the rod and reel. Who knows, you might make a strike next time and bring home 200 pounds (90 kg) of amethyst. It's fun anyway and if your hunting is not successful you can always buy the materials later.

Those living in the West and near the Mexican border always have a source of tumbling materials nearby. Fine agates and petrified wood, plus many other interesting stones, are abundant in these locales and the tumbling hobby so popular that many sites are common knowledge. Those of us in the rest of the country may not be so lucky. How do we find the amethysts?

Fig. 2-1 Quarries may be good sources of tumbling materials.

GEM-HUNTING GUIDES

Not, unfortunately, with the gem-hunting guides that entice so many at mineral displays and bookstores. These guides will generate a severe case of rock fever with their accounts of the fisherman who found a pocket of amethysts under a tree root; the boy who picked up a glistening white pebble that turned out to be a 20-carat diamond; or the picnickers who stumbled upon a hundred thousand dollars worth of green tourmaline. All the stories are true, but no book will enable a prospector to duplicate them; what's required for that is pure dumb luck.

Some books are better than others. Over the years we have found that about one-quarter of the sites listed, on the average, still have *something* to offer. The others are buried under garbage dumps—a very popular use for old mines—in the middle of housing developments; or are so lost and overgrown that they can't be found. This is not the fault of the guide's author. No human being could possibly visit all the sites in a single state and, therefore, many of the gem-hunting locations are based on geologists' reports dating back to the middle of the last century. There may have been beryl crystals at a particular location in 1853, but a lot has happened since then. Furthermore, if the site is listed in a book which several thousand other people have bought, at least some of them must have been there, too; if there is anything left on location it will require a lot of digging.

Locating and Choosing Tumbling Materials 9

MINERALOGICAL SOCIETIES

What to do? By all means use a gem-hunting guide if you like pirate treasure, but be prepared for disappointment at least three out of four times. While you pursue these chimeras, send in your six dollars for a membership in the local mineralogical society. It's worth every penny. These people know where the *current* sites are. During field trips you can prospect in the company of experts, who will tell you what to look for and where.

Before going on vacation, it may be a good idea to gather your own information by writing to the secretary of the mineralogical society in the area you're to visit, giving your vacation address and the type of minerals you are looking for. Many societies will send a map of prospecting areas within a 50-mile (80-kilometer) radius. The names and addresses of chapter secretaries are listed annually in the *Lapidary Journal*. (The April buyers' guide of this magazine will also list the rock shops along the way.)

Since this book is devoted primarily to tumbling, we can only give a few hints about locating your own materials. More comprehensive instructions are provided in books dealing with mineral collecting, but this is no substitute for experience. You can learn by trial and error, but the process will be much faster and more satisfying if you go out a few times with an expert and learn his methods. Rock hunting, like fishing, is always a matter of luck, but the best fortune generally comes to the prospector who knows what he's doing.

ROCK SHOPS AND ROCKHOUNDS

Owners of rock shops started out as collectors, and are as cognizant of the economics of prospecting as anyone else. They also love the business and are mines of information. Make it a point to stop and talk with them en route. Paradoxically, the rock shop owner will often provide direction to the best locations for finding the very minerals he sells.

Other sources of information include the list of guides in *Rocks and Minerals* and the traders' section of the same magazine. Traders are simply other collectors who wish to exchange materials. If you visit them on home ground, they are often willing to guide you on local collecting trips.

PROSPECTING

Once you have located a site, take time to look around and familiarize yourself with the lay of the land. Don't start knocking boulders or digging right away. The time you spend intelligently can save hours of hard and fruitless labor. Probably most of the good material will have been picked off the surface. See if you can find where it came from. A sample of the

Fig. 2-2 Tumbling materials often occur in veins, seen in quarry faces or in road cuts where the rock strata are exposed.

material to be found at the location will help—another reason for stopping at a rock shop if one is handy.

If the mineral occurs in a vein, it may be difficult to get material out without removing large quantities of country rock. It is a good idea to look for other outcroppings or to dig down from the surface in hope of hitting the vein further on. If the material occurs in a certain type of formation, don't waste time on formations that look different. Pockets of some materials occur in regular geometric patterns (Fig. 2-2). Try to find the one that fits.

The beginner can often obtain good results simply by playing follow the leader. The best collecting spots are where other people have dug. Look for the location with the most holes, find a piece of virgin territory if you can, and stake out your claim. The earlier holes will also indicate how deep and in what direction you will have to dig for the material.

Locating and Choosing Tumbling Materials 11

Once you have chosen a location to dig (and digging is the only way to find fresh material if the surface has been picked over), stick with it. Don't change holes, even if the people 20 feet (6 meters) away have struck it rich.

For this type of collecting, you will need a mason's hammer—all metal and more practical than the geologist's pick; a sledge hammer; assorted chisels; a shovel; a large steel slice bar. Don't ever try to use a claw hammer for cracking rocks. The claws will fly off first, then pieces of the face, with the velocity of bullets. Wear safety glasses even with tools meant for the job.

Surface collecting is less wearing, but this can be done only in a limited number of areas, such as stream beds or old mine dumps. You will need a small sledge, or cracking, hammer to break the rocks in order to examine the internal faces.

Road cuts are another good source of tumbling materials, since veins and their directions are clearly exposed. After you have been collecting for a while, you'll probably carry a hammer in the car at all times and find yourself looking for colors in rock faces on every turnpike.

When you're through, try to leave the site in good condition, free from trash and if possible, with some material for the next collector. If you are in a major collecting location, used only for rock hunting, you do not need to fill in the hole; in fact, you'll be saving someone else work by indicating a

Fig. 2-3 A fundamental rule of rock collecting is to leave some for other prospectors.

Fig. 2-4 Always wear a hard hat and stay away from badly fractured walls, such as these.

Locating and Choosing Tumbling Materials 13

site that's already been excavated. But in the woods or fields, filling in is a must if the site is to remain open to collectors. In a quarry, keep an inventory of your tools and don't leave until every one has been accounted for. A chisel can ruin a rock crusher. Follow the quarry's safety rules, including the wearing of hard hats, and stay away from vertical or overhanging rock faces (Fig. 2-4). You'll see why if you stand quietly for a few moments and listen to the stones falling from the top of the face.

To many people, collecting is half the fun of rock tumbling. It provides good outdoor exercise, usually in congenial company, with all the incentive of treasure hunting. It leads them into all kinds of unusual locations, some fascinating, some dismal, some beautiful, but all interesting. And there is the added bonus of being able to take the results home, put them in a machine and produce something of value. For what it's worth, prospectors—if they wear hard hats and don't fall off cliffs—seem to live forever. Or, as the plaques in the rock shops point out: "Old rockhounds never die, they just slowly petrify."

Chapter 3

Selecting and Preparing Tumbling Materials

HARDNESS

There are a number of qualities to look for in rough materials, whether found or bought. One of these qualities is *hardness*. In addition to indicating a degree of polishability, hardness is also a primary means of mineral identification. The Mohs scale of hardness is the most generally accepted measure: the scale is not a straight-line relationship, but a curve that rises rapidly for stones of high hardness values. Thus diamond, at 10, is several thousand times harder than synthetic materials at 9.5. A rough and ready test can be made with the common materials shown on the scale, the material on any given level will scratch any material below it. Human skin has a hardness of about 1.5.

Mohs Scale of Hardness

1. Talc
2. Gypsum
3. Calcite—Human fingernail, 2½, will scratch talc or gypsum
4. Fluorite
5. Apatite—Similar to bone in hardness and composition
6. Orthoclase—Knife blade, 6½, will scratch any material below 6
7. Quartz
8. Topaz
9. Corundum—Tumbling abrasive
10. Diamond

Selecting and Preparing Tumbling Materials

Hardness has an additional importance in rock tumbling, since every stone in a batch must have the same degree of hardness if polishing is to be successful.

TYPE OF FRACTURE

Stones are also classified by type of *fracture*. Most tumbling material will have one of three characteristic modes: brittle, conchoidal (Fig. 3-1), or along cleavage planes.

An irregular, grainy fracture generally means that the material does not have sufficient structural integrity for satisfactory tumbling. Hard, amorphous materials, such as jasper or obsidian, have conchoidal fractures, in which the broken ends of a piece will have a glossy surface, curved like a seashell. Crystalline materials, such as amazonite or "sunstone" feldspars, will fracture cleanly along cleavage planes, or lines of structural weakness in the material. Stones of this type will often show further cleavage during tumbling and will have to be returned to the first grind unless great care is taken when breaking up the rough. Some material, such as a rose quartz or amethyst, if roughly handled or exposed to wide temperature variations, is subject to multiple fracturing. In this case the material, instead of being glasslike and clear, will have a multitude of hairline cracks. The stone may break or chip along one of these lines in

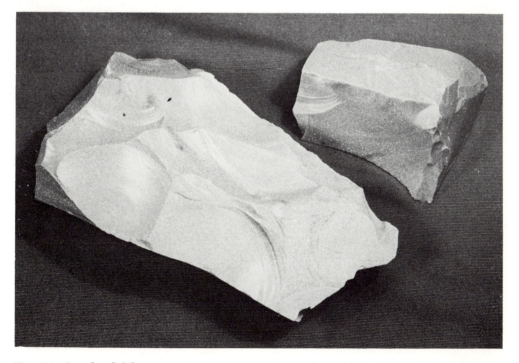

Fig. 3-1 Conchoidal fracturing is common to many rock tumbling materials, including the goldstone shown here.

tumbling, but more importantly, the stone, even if perfectly polished, will still look like a fried marble. Discard any material with multiple fractures unless you want it for special effect and you're willing to risk the polish of the other stones in the batch.

Softer stones, such as turquoise or malachite, can also be given a fine polish by tumbling, but require special techniques to be described later. Even soft metals, such as silver or copper, can be tumble polished with excellent results. Some jewelry makers tumble batches of silver with steel shot to obtain a beautiful satin finish with a fraction of the labor required for hand polishing (see Ch. 14).

GRAIN AND PITTING

After hardness and fracture of the material have been tested, it should be checked for *grain and pitting*. This is especially important when you do not know exactly what type of stone you are working with, often the case with material such as beach pebbles. Coarse, sandy grain will not polish; some of the shiny pebbles you see on the beach may have this kind of grain internally. Pitting is more insidious, often occurring as small voids

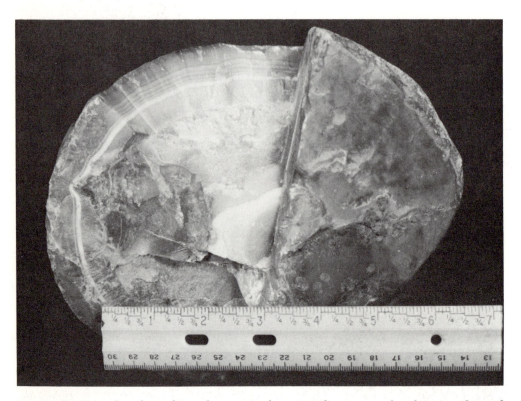

Fig. 3-2 Fractured surface of Brazilian agate shows good integrity, cleanliness, color and banding. Purchased materials should be examined carefully along fresh fractures.

Selecting and Preparing Tumbling Materials

in otherwise sound rock. Pitted stones, besides looking bad, will prevent other stones in the batch from polishing, since grit from previous abrasive steps will be trapped in the pits and escape to ruin the next step. If you cannot break up the material finely enough to avoid *all* pitting, throw it away. It is a good idea to spot-check fractured surfaces with a magnifying glass. An exception is the "rind" of such materials as amethystine geodes, which may be covered with a soft porous material easily worn away in the rough grinding stage. In this case the material should be examined for pitting after the first tumbling step.

COLOR AND INCLUSIONS

When prospecting or purchasing, try for colorful material. You are going to spend six weeks or so polishing it, so choose a color you like and one which will be attractive when polished. Wetting the fractured surface will show the finished color and also bring out fine detail which may not be noticeable when the stone is dry.

After prospecting, you are bound to try tumbling some material for sentimental reasons. When we first began rock hunting, we would try to polish anything, if only to prove that a trip hadn't been a total loss. Once near Unionville, Pennsylvania, looking in a garbage dump for corundum crystals, we found some jasper, as solid and fine grained as glass. It took a beautiful polish. The only drawback was its drab brown color, without the slightest banding or other interest. When we were finished we had a well-polished batch of mud-brown rocks. They wound up on the bottom of the fish tank.

Wet the surface and imagine the finished material with the eye of a critic, rather than that of a proud father. Wetting the surface will also show invisible fractures, which will appear as dark lines after the rest of the surface dries. Some dull-colored material is retrieved by bands, dots or *inclusions* (other minerals), or by translucency. Everyone to his own taste. Some people will call a color scheme dull while others will find it full of subtlety. Maguey agate, purplish brown with white cometlike streaks, is one example. Some people like it, some don't.

The included material, dots, streaks or bands, must be integral with the base material and of approximately the same hardness for good results. For example, small pyrite (fool's gold) inclusions in blue sodalite polish very well and add to the attractiveness of the stone, since the two materials are of similar hardness. Softer inclusions will wear away faster than the base stone and cause pitting or, if only slightly softer, will polish before the base. Large inclusions will probably separate from the rest of the stone during tumbling.

Some of the more interesting patterned stones are snowflake obsidian, Brazilian banded agate, "eye" agate, lace agate and malachite.

Fig. 3-3 The base material in this piece of tiger-eye rough is clean and free of fractures.

CLEANLINESS

Probably the most important characteristic of any tumbling material is what can loosely be described as *cleanness*. After seeing the results of a few batches you will soon get a feel for it. The rough will be clean, hard and all-of-a-piece (Fig. 3-3). The final result will be inherent from the start.

Part of your good feeling about the material will come from remembering the cardinal rule of tumbling, one that beginners tend to forget. The rule is the same one that applies to computer programming: GIGO. Or, *garbage in–garbage out*. The tumbler is not a magic device for turning road gravel into precious stones. The final gem must be inherent in the original material, in its shape, its hardness and its coloration. If you remember this you may have some mishaps and have to start again from the beginning, but eventually you will get extremely satisfying results. On the other hand, if you throw something in and hope for the best you are going to be disappointed. This is the point that relegates so many tumbling machines to the attic after one or two uses. Any machine described in this book will produce beautiful results, but only if used properly and with a knowledge of its limitations.

Selecting and Preparing Tumbling Materials 19

Fig. 3-4 A convenient means for storing a piece of porous rough.

CHARACTERISTICS OF PURCHASED MATERIALS

The same rules apply to purchased materials as to found materials. If you buy from a reputable supplier, at least part of the work—locating the best material in the vein—should have been done for you.

You will certainly want to purchase at least some of your material from mail-order houses, if only to try out some gemstones unavailable in your own area. Tumbling material varies widely in price. Good quality amethyst, at the time of writing, sells for about $6 to $8 per pound (0.4 kg), yellow jasper $.75 to $1.50 per pound, and the best quality Mexican lace agate for $3.50 per pound. You may be surprised at first by what seem to be low prices for semiprecious stones. This is an illusion. A few batches of tumbling rough will probably cost more than your tumbler and all its ancillary equipment combined. Then you will have to tumble the stones at least six weeks; in each of four grinds you will lose a certain percentage through breakage and attrition. When you are finished you will find yourself setting a more realistic value on each polished stone.

Some of the major sources of tumbling rough are listed in trade magazines such as the *Lapidary Journal*. These range from full-scale mining operations to rockhounds who have collected more material than they need. Commercial sources for rough vary almost as much as collecting locations. This might be expected, since new prospects are opened up all the time and as one material goes out of fashion something else takes its place. The best way to learn what is "in" at the moment, where to get it and what it looks like is by attending local mineral shows.

When ordering by mail, try to get a sample first. Most suppliers will be willing to send you a few pieces for inspection. If you decide to order, you will probably find that the material you receive is as good as or better than the sample. This is because most miners are afraid of "highgrading" their samples (choosing only the good pieces) and disappointing customers later. They will deliberately choose the most average specimens as samples.

The vast majority of dealers in minerals for tumbling give good value for the money since they want repeat customers, but there are always some willing to prey on the unwary. Beware of bargains. You get what you pay for with rocks as with anything else, and material that sells for much below the going rate probably just isn't as good. If you become a large consumer and order a batch of new material, you can probably work out a deal whereby you pay only after inspection of the merchandise. As a hobbyist you have very little recourse save the characteristic American one of keeping your mouth shut and going elsewhere. Try to get materials mailed COD; always pay by check and make sure the supplier pays the freight (both ways if you're dissatisfied). A half ton of boulders from Mexico takes a lot of stamps.

Selecting and Preparing Tumbling Materials

SELECTING QUALITY BEACH PEBBLES

On the subject of materials, a few words about beach pebbles are in order. They are the reason many people buy their first rock tumbler—to try to recapture the beauty of sea-wet stones when back inland after a vacation. Tumblers are sold in many shore resorts; unfortunately, vacationers are often disappointed with the results. Of course, nothing can capture the atmosphere of sun, sand and surf where the pebbles were first seen and collected, but many times the final stone does not even have the water-wet sheen that made it so attractive in the first place. It should! A tumble-polished gemstone should look exactly the same wet or dry. This is the best test of final polish, as we will see when we reach that step; it is also the reason to persist with your beach pebbles. It can be done.

One would seem to be starting with an advantage when tumbling beach pebbles. The surfaces have been rounded and smoothed by the waves into pleasing shapes, and it looks as if the first step in tumbling—rough grinding to round down the sharp edges—has already been done. There are two things to watch out for, though.

The first is that sand and wave action can smooth granite or sandstone to the point where it looks polished when wet. The process can't be taken any further. Leave these coarse-grained stones on the beach for others to admire. You may have to break a few open to find the stuff of which they are made.

The second is the tendency to collect stones that are roughly the same in size and shape, with a preponderance of larger pebbles. As will be seen later, successful tumbling requires at least some variety in the size of the rough pieces.

For the rest, treat beach pebbles as you would any other material. Select them on the basis of interesting color or pattern and make sure that all the stones in each batch are of the same material or, at the very least, of the same hardness. Don't try a coarse-grained piece just to see what will happen. It will pick up abrasive material from the previous batch and ruin the rest of your stones.

You can usually rely on wave action for the rough grind if pieces are sized on the basis of the recommendations given below. If the pebbles have surface fractures or unwanted unevenness, you will have to start at the beginning.

The waves were the first tumbler. Perhaps it was from the ocean that man first got the idea of polishing rocks. There are beaches on both the Atlantic and Pacific coasts where most of the pebbles are semiprecious stones like jasper. If you visit such a site, all you will have to do is finish what the waves have begun.

Chapter 4

Equipment and Workshop Requirements

Compared to many other hobbies, rock tumbling is inexpensive to begin. The smallest tumbling machines, if properly selected and used, will provide results comparable to those obtainable with the largest professional units.

Since small tumbling machines are so cheap, it is a good idea to buy the best available in the size range that interests you. The rough gem material and abrasive costs, over a relatively short period of time, will amount to far more than what was spent originally on the machine.

SMALL TUMBLERS

For purposes of comparison, small tumblers are those with barrels that accept from 3 to 6 pounds (1.4 to 2.7 kg) of rock. They are generally driven by a small fan motor developing about 1/20 horsepower (0.37 kw) and consuming from 35 to 50 watts, about the same as a dim light bulb. Good single-barrel units, at the time of writing, sell for $10 to $15. Double-barrel machines run from $19 to $23. For reasons that will be explained later, we recommend a double-barrel tumbler.

What to Look For

The tumbler barrel or barrels in a small unit should be made of solid rubber (Fig. 4-1). Some of the tumbling kits on the market include a plastic barrel with a rubber liner. Although such tumblers will give satisfactory

Equipment and Workshop Requirements 23

Fig. 4-1 The best small tumblers are equipped with solid rubber barrels. (Star Diamond Industries, Inc.)

results for a few batches, the barrel will wear out rapidly and, before it does, its outside surface will become polished in spots. Practically all rotary tumblers consist of a cylindrical barrel resting on two shafts, either or both of which are driven. The motion of the shafts is communicated to the barrel by friction. Thus, if either the barrel or the shaft becomes polished, the friction drive is lost and the barrel turns irregularly or not at all, like a tire spinning on an icy patch.

The seal on a plastic barrel, usually simply a jar lid with a rubber liner, also leaves something to be desired. If is difficult to get a tight seal; abrasives have a way of getting into the threads and under the seal where they are almost impossible to remove.

The all-rubber barrel, on the other hand, will last four to five years in continuous operation, is easy to clean, retains its frictional properties, and has a threadless seal that seldom leaks.

The drive motor itself seldom presents a problem on any tumbler.

Fig. 4-2 A good example of a complete, self-contained small tumbler with a rubber barrel.

Over the years, little fan motors have become extremely reliable. They run hot—from 40° to 55° F (4.4°–12.8° C) above ambient temperature—so don't worry if your tumbler feels hot to the touch after running for a time.

More important is the drive mechanism. Many small tumblers have been made with a rubber O ring to serve as the drive belt between the motor pulley and the tumbler drive shaft. Such O rings stretch rapidly and, although there may be an adjustment to take up the slack, it will soon reach its farthest limit and the drive will begin to slip. These belts soon crack in various places and the cracks develop into a complete break.

The best type of drive for a small tumbler is a replaceable V belt on standard pulleys. Such belts generally last from twelve to eighteen months and can be replaced easily if necessary.

The two drive shafts on which the barrel rests are covered with rubber or plastic to increase friction and set in plastic bearings at each end. Although plastic bearings are said to require no lubrication, we have found that they do run more freely if lubricated periodically with a few drops of light machine oil. On new bearings, such lubrication might cause the plastic to swell and bind the shaft, but after the machine has been running

Equipment and Workshop Requirements

for a time, oiling does reduce friction, as measured by the power consumption of the drive motor. It is also important to keep the tumbler clean to prevent particles of abrasive from working their way into the bearings.

The drive rod surface may become polished after a few months, especially if any of the material in the tumbler leaks onto the shafts, and may have to be sanded lightly to restore friction.

As the best compromise between cost and performance, we recommend a tumbler with two 3-pound (1.4 kg) rubber barrels, similar to the Scott-Murray machine or the Lortone 3NR. The upper limit for the hobbyist just starting out should be a unit with two 12-pound (5.4-kg) barrels. Whatever unit you buy, invest in a spare barrel: $3 for 3-pound capacity (1.4 kg) to $10 for 12-pound capacity (5.4 kg). Use the spare unit for the polishing step. This will eliminate the single most common cause of poorly polished stones: carry-over of abrasive from the prepolish to the polish step.

Why Two Barrels?

A two-barrel unit costs little more than a single-barrel tumbler, provides greater flexibility, and saves time. For example, in the section on procedures, it will be noted that the tumbler must be *at least* half full, but less than three-quarters full, for the correct tumbling action to take place. Now in the rough grind step, about 20 to 25 percent of volume will be lost. Thus, if the rough grind started with the container five-eighths full, the next step may already be close to the lower limit for effective tumbling. If one starts with two barrels full in rough grind, there will be ample material

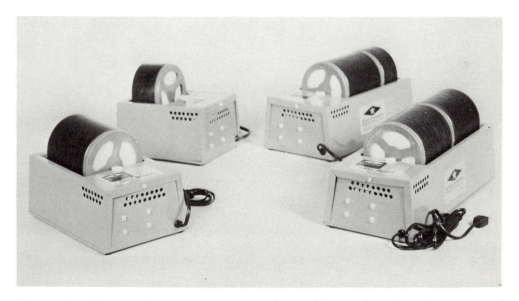

Fig. 4-3 Tumbler manufacturers, recognizing the need for two barrels, make a variety of units. Shown here are barrels with capacities of 1½, 3, 3 and 1½, and 6 pounds (0.67, 1.4, 1.4 and 0.67, and 2.7 kg). (Star Diamond Industries, Inc.)

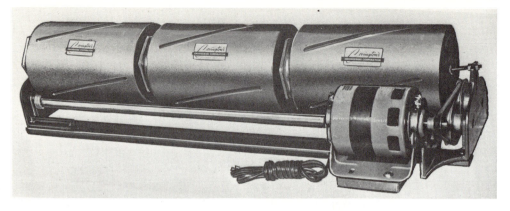

Fig. 4-4 A triple-barrel tumbler. This machine is available in sizes with 9 to 36 pound (4.05–16.20 kg) total capacity. Note the O-ring drive. (Covington Engineering Corp.)

left to fill one of the barrels to an effective level for the next step, while the other barrel can be charged for another rough grind. The final results will probably be better, not only because the tumbling levels will be correct, but also because the hobbyist will be able to select the best stones from both batches to begin the second step, without worrying about whether he has enough material to fill the tumbler.

Small tumbling barrels have advantages even for the professional. During rotation the mass of tumbling stones climbs part way up the inner wall of the tumbler, then rolls or slides back to begin the process again. In a small tumbler the stones have less potential energy to be transformed into kinetic energy as they reach the base of the mass; thus, the action is less likely to chip or mar delicate edges or shapes. This can be helpful in tumbling *preforms*—shapes such as crosses or hearts sawed and rough ground from a stone slab and then tumble polished.

MEDIUM-SIZED TUMBLERS

For the purposes discussed in this book, medium tumblers are those with single or multiple barrels each with a capacity of 6 to 12 pounds (2.7–5.4 kg). Such machines are still within range of the hobbyist, and are most popular among those who make some polished stone jewelry for sale. They will produce a reasonable number of saleable stones without swamping a small shop by overproduction.

Medium-sized tumblers operate on exactly the same principles as smaller ones, but are more likely to have V-belt drive and a somewhat larger motor. Single-barrel units generally use a 35 to 60-watt fan motor; a triple-barrel tumbler, each barrel holding 12 pounds (5.4 kg), uses a ¼ horsepower (.186 kw) motor consuming from 300 to 600 watts, depending upon load (about 5 amperes at idle). Prices range from $32 to $40 for a single barrel to $70 to $110 for a triple 12.

Equipment and Workshop Requirements

Fig. 4-5 A typical tumbler employing a steel shell with a hexagonal rubber liner. This medium-sized tumbler comes in sizes up to 12 pounds (5.4 kg) capacity per barrel. (Star Diamond Industries, Inc.)

Barrels in this size range may be either solid rubber or hexagonal steel containers with rubber liners. The hexagonal shape (Fig. 4-5) is said to improve tumbling action—although we have found that round barrels produce equally good results. The surface that rides on the drive bars, however, remains cylindrical and may be rubber coated to improve friction.

The triple 12 is probably the most popular unit among serious hobbyists because it increases the multiple barrel flexibility described earlier. Three batches of stones may be processed at the same time, each batch of different hardness or each in different stages of processing. The amount of finished stones produced in a given period of time is greatly increased, since a new batch of rough may be started while an earlier batch is undergoing the polishing step. (We will be recommending a four-step tumbling process for all materials, with the possible exception of graded beach pebbles.)

The standard, off-the-shelf model of a triple 12 has only one disadvantage. The three barrels all rest on the same pair of drive shafts. They are

Figs. 4-6, 4-7 Medium-sized single-shaft tumblers. This design is said to give "triple" tumbling action because of the angle of the shaft and the barrel design. The primary advantage of such tumblers is that the load can be checked without removing the tumbler barrel from the machine. (Ferrara Industries, Inc.)

Equipment and Workshop Requirements

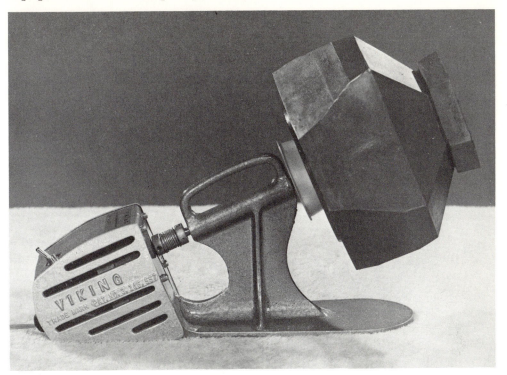

Fig. 4-8 Another medium-sized single-shaft tumbler. (Geode Industries, Inc.)

centered on the shafts by plastic tabs or buffer pads that keep the barrels from colliding with the bearings at the ends. The plastic tabs wear out much sooner than one would imagine. The result is a scored tumbler barrel or the grinding away of the nuts that fasten the tops of the barrels. The plastic tabs may be replaced with pieces of Masonite soaked in oil: these seem to wear longer, with less friction, than the plastic.

Fig. 4-9 Most tumbler manufacturers make a complete line of units, from small to medium in size, with either all-rubber barrels or steel barrels with rubber liners. (Star Diamond Industries, Inc.)

For best results, both shafts on this type of unit should be driven. This is usually done by means of sheaves and a running belt between the two shafts. To accomplish the tumbling of difficult materials, it is also a good idea to equip the drive motor with a pulley having at least two sheaves of different diameter, so that the speed of rotation of the tumbler can be varied if necessary. Many ¼-horsepower (.186 kw) motors now have two speeds, which will serve the same purpose more conveniently. This type of motor costs more and must be equipped with a double-pole–double-throw switch to permit speed selection without rewiring.

LARGE TUMBLERS

The lapidary hobbyist, no matter how advanced, will seldom have a need for any unit over 75-pound (33.75-kg) capacity—three 25-pound (11.25-kg) barrels—but commercial units may be as large as 3,500 pounds (1575 kg). The 25-pound units are available commercially from a number of small manufacturers or individual craftsmen at prices ranging from $60 to $100, but in this size range it is probably more economical to build your own.

A triple 25 can be built easily from scrap angle iron, steel shafts covered with automobile radiator hose, commercial pillow block bearings, sheaves and a ⅓-horsepower (.249 kw) motor. Barrels are available separately from manufacturers who advertise in magazines such as the *Lapidary Journal*. A homebuilt tumbler, as described in Chapter 5, may not be more economical, but it can incorporate features, such as sealed ball bearings, not found in most commercial units. The break-even point for building versus buying occurs at a tumbler size of about 36 pounds (16.2 kg). Economics aside, a well-built do-it-yourself unit may prove more sound mechanically in the long run.

SETTING UP A WORKSHOP

Once you have selected or built a tumbler, find the best place to put it. Some people find the constant swishing of a tumbler as soothing as the sound of a mountain stream; others do not. Therefore, try to find a place where neither you nor your neighbors will be bothered by the noise.

The basement, if you have one, is usually the best place for a tumbler. It is far enough from the rest of the house so that the noise will not be noticeable and it usually has the other requirements for setting up a rock-tumbling workshop.

Necessities are a source of running water, including a sink if possible, power, good lighting, a solid area for breaking up rocks, storage space and someplace to dispose of used grit.

The tumbler can also be put in the garage, but in northern climates,

Equipment and Workshop Requirements

unless the garage is heated, antifreeze will have to be used in the winter to prevent the mass of stones and water from freezing. Stones can be tumbled efficiently in propylene glycol, if necessary.

To take the requirements in order, running water is a necessity for filling the tumbler and, more important, for thorough cleaning of the stones between tumbling stages. An old stone sink once used for clothes washing is ideal for detergent cleaning of stones. It has plenty of room to spread them out and is deep enough to prevent splashes. For washing use a plastic collander (aluminum marks the stones).

Disposing of residue from tumbling can be a problem. The used abrasive and rock dust form a thick solution that can set like cement when it dries, clogging any bends in drain pipes. The residue from the rough grind, at least, should either be buried or allowed to dry and spread lightly on the lawn. The materials are all natural, nontoxic and relatively inert, and will do no harm to the environment.

Residue from subsequent stages of tumbling will not contain as much powdered stone and can be washed down the drain if accompanied by copious amounts of water. To be on the safe side, dispose of the solution from the first *two* stages outdoors.

Normal house current on a 15-amp fuse will be more than adequate for most rock tumbling. Since the process involves a water solution, the tumbler should always be grounded, either with a standard three-prong plug or, if this type of plug does not come with the tumbler, a ground wire leading from the metal frame of the tumbler to a pipe buried in the ground or some other safe grounding connection.

Good lighting is a necessity for inspecting your stones. The best lighted area should be near the sink, so the stones can be sorted as they are washed. It should be high in intensity but glare-free for evaluation of the final polish.

We recommend the basement also because it generally has a solid concrete floor, and a solid surface is needed for breaking up rough material. This can be done directly on the concrete, but it will rapidly break up the floor surface as well as the stones. A better surface is a ½-inch (12.7-mm) or thicker steel plate or anvil about a foot square. The plate should rest on a thin insulating pad of newspapers laid on the concrete to absorb shock and prevent the plate from bouncing all over the room. You will need two hammers for cracking rock: a short-handled sledge hammer with at least a 16-ounce (.4-kg) head and a smaller mason's hammer or geologist's pick. *Under no circumstances should an ordinary claw hammer be used*. Actual breaking and sorting procedures will be described in a later section, but be assured that you will be breaking up some of the world's toughest material. It will pay to have plenty of firepower in the form of heavy, top quality equipment. For cracking, a pair of gloves and safety glasses are also a necessity.

For the tumbler itself, a firm, solid surface is required to minimize noise and vibration. Most larger tumblers are simply mounted on the floor, but smaller ones can be put on a solid workbench to make changing barrels more convenient.

The last requisite for an efficient tumbling setup is plenty of storage space, preferably with bins that can be identified as to contents. Whoever gets at all involved in the hobby will eventually collect an amazing variety of material. It will pay to know where everything is, especially since effective tumbling depends upon every stone in the batch being of equal composition or hardness. Bins or shelves should be made as sturdy as possible because of the weight of material.

Bulk rough materials usually come in burlap bags. Leave the stones in the bags until ready for use to avoid mixups. A good way to store polished stones is in transparent plastic boxes, since the stones can be located easily by color. File cabinets with plastic box compartments can be purchased inexpensively and are a good investment.

SUPPLIES

Abrasive Materials

The selection of abrasives is critical to good rock tumbling. The most common abrasive for tumbling is silicon carbide for the coarser stages. This is available in tumbling kits or can be purchased in quantities of one pound (.4 kg) or more at rock and hobby shops. The price differential between kit materials and those loosely packed is insignificant unless you buy in quantities larger than 10 pounds (4.5 kg) in each grit size. The polishing kit abrasives are satisfactory if they are for a four-step process; the three-step kits lack an abrasive. Most kits nowadays are four-step. The three-step units have a 100-mesh abrasive, a 600-mesh and a polish; the stones are not sufficiently ground in any reasonable length of time to be ready for the polish step. (The higher the mesh number, the finer the abrasive.) Three-step tumbling is possible if the stones are run in each step at least 50 percent longer than is called for in the kit instructions.

Loose abrasives allow you to choose the right type of abrasive for the stone hardness you are working with. For most purposes (and the tumbling recommendations provided in this book) you should stock a 100-mesh, a 220 or 320 (3F), a 400 and a 600. The prepolish is usually Tripoli or some similar material. The polish itself is the main reason we recommend buying loose material rather than a kit. The packaged kit often contains a polish that is not suitable for some stones. A red hematite polish, for example, gets into natural fractures in stones such as rose quartz or the feldspars and emphasizes these flaws to the extent that the polished stone is unusable. Such polishes work well, however, on fine-grained materials such as agates.

Abrasives do not deteriorate in storage, but in damp places they will absorb moisture and cake, making them difficult to get out of the container and to measure. In damp basements they can be stored in plastic contain-

Equipment and Workshop Requirements

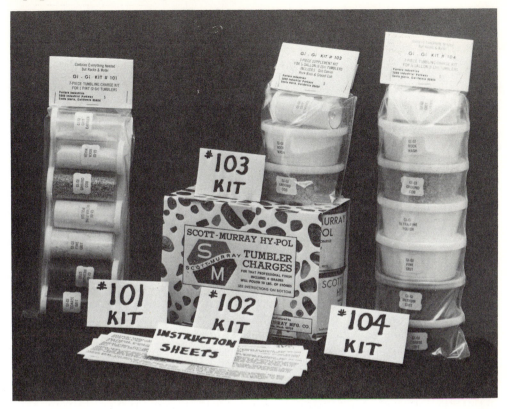

Fig. 4-10 Prepackaged kits contain all the abrasive materials necessary for processing.

ers or in the paper-board drums in which they are sold, as long as these are raised above floor level.

Buffering Agents

Some other supplies you should have on hand include buffering materials. These are used after the roughing stages to carry the abrasive and also to prevent severe impact of one stone against another, which could cause chipping and prevent polishing entirely. Such materials include wood chips, plastic pellets, sawdust, sugar and wallpaper paste. Their use is described in the section containing recommendations for various hardness of material. One quality to be looked for is flotation. If *all* the material floats to the top when the stones are washed, it is easy to separate from the batch. If some of its sinks and mixes with the stones, separation can become a very messy problem.

There are also products on the market, such as Tumble-Trol (made by Geode Industries, Inc.) that increase the viscosity of the solution and reduce the force of impact. The use of one of these "tumbling pills" or sugar is a must when tumbling difficult materials such as Apache Tears. Wallpaper paste is another possibility for thickening.

You will also need soap powder to wash the stones, to add to the

Fig. 4-11 Typical quantities of all materials required to process 10 pounds (4.5 kg) of rock.

tumbling solution in rotary tumblers, to thicken it and increase its wetting action, and to use as a final tumbling step with water after polishing to remove all traces of polish. Baking soda is added to most tumblers to prevent gas formation. Gas formation is a problem with some type of materials. Goldstone, an artificial stone made in Italy and containing millions of flecks of gold-colored copper, for some reason or other is a particularly good gas generator. Without the use of baking soda, it will cause a solid rubber tumbler to blow up like a balloon.

Old-timers often had their own favorite additives, which helped to make rock tumbling a mysterious art. These included products such as walnut shells, rice hulls and even banana peels. Although such things may work, we don't recommend using them; first, because the amounts are uncontrollable; second, because bacterial action in the tumbler may make your workshop smell like the clam flats at low tide.

Chapter 5

Building Your Own Tumbler

At any price range over $35, it becomes economical to build your own tumbler. This chapter contains all the design information necessary to construct tumblers up to 200 pounds (90 kg) total capacity—more than enough for the most ambitious noncommercial shop. A homemade machine can incorporate, at no extra cost, quality features not found on commercial units.

CONSTRUCTION SUPPLIES

Everyone has his own particular requirements of a tumbling machine; thus, we have not specified any particular size or method of construction, but merely supplied the design calculations necessary to build a tumbler that works. The description in this chapter provides some construction hints based on experience, but you may have better ideas.

Frame Construction

The framing for the machine should be of 2 x 4s (50.8 x 101.6 mm lumber) or heavier material, fastened together with lag bolts. Strong construction is necessary to keep the shafts running true, especially if large-capacity tumbler barrels are to be supported.

The strongest and most convenient frame, if the hobbyist has access to welding equipment, can be made from angle iron (available cheaply from a scrap yard). All that is required, no matter what the method of construction, is a rectangular frame (usually on legs) of sufficient length and width to suit the tumbler barrel and shaft dimensions chosen from the calculations. The frame's sole purpose is to support four pillow block bearings in which the barrel drive shafts are mounted.

If desired, the tumbler can be made without a frame at all, by mounting the pillow blocks directly on a heavy table, making sure the shafts are raised high enough to prevent the section of the barrel between them from rubbing on the tabletop.

If a tabletop is used, the shafts must extend beyond the edge so that the drive sheave (pulley) can be attached. The motor can be mounted on a hinged board directly beneath. The weight of the motor provides the proper tension on the drive belt.

Pillow Blocks and Bearings

Pillow blocks are available from any bearing supply house at moderate cost. They should be equipped with sealed ball bearings for long-term, trouble-free operation. Most commercial tumblers have plastic sleeve bearings that require too much attention to keep them running free; plastic also wears out rather rapidly. Thus, good bearings are one important advantage of the homemade unit. Since a tumbler runs at low speed, bearings could also be made from wood (oiled oak or good multilayered plywood), but sealed ball bearings are so inexpensive that the difference in cost for the tumbler as a whole would be minimal. Bearing size is based on the required shaft diameter as chosen from Table 2.

Speed Control

Another advantage of a do-it-yourself tumbler is speed control. Reducing speed 25% to 35% in the prepolish and polish stages prevents damage to stones and produces a better finish without the amounts of additives required when using a single-speed tumbler. (The figures above are for a round barrel; a hexagonal barrel requires a 20% to 30% speed reduction.) The most accurate speed reduction can be achieved by a double sheave—one small and one large—on the tumbler drive shaft (see Tables 1 and 2 and sample calculations for the required sheave size).

For round barrels, a standard (1750 and 1180 rpm) two-speed motor provides almost exactly the required speed reduction. All you need in this case is a double-pole–double-throw switch connected to the high and low-speed windings of the motor. This is wired in accordance with instructions that come with the switch or printed on the motor plate.

Barrels

We have not included tumbler barrels in the design considerations (although these could also be homemade) since good barrels, up to 25-pound (11.25-kg) capacity, are available on the market at lower cost than anything that could be made in the shop, when one considers the difficulty of rubber lining and sealing. We definitely recommend rubber liners; unlined containers will present all sorts of unforeseen difficulties and will

Building Your Own Tumbler

wear out very rapidly. So unless you have an unlimited supply of sealable paint cans, use rubber-lined barrels.

The basic tumbler design can be expanded to almost any size, with up to four barrels, another advantage, since the 25-pound (11.25-kg) unit on the market has only a single barrel. Remember, however, that a large tumbler will consume considerable amounts of rough material, all of which must be broken and carefully sorted.

Materials for the homemade tumbler are available at hardware stores, bearing supply houses, and junkyards: pillow blocks, bearings, frame materials, shafts, motor, sheaves and belts. Remember to buy the sheaves and the belts at the same time. The drive belt and sheave must match. A type A belt requires a type A sheave, and the supplier will provide the correct type automatically if the items are purchased together.

Drive Shafts and Sheaves

For better friction, the drive shafts are covered with radiator hose having an inside diameter equal to the shaft diameter. It may be difficult to get the tubing on the shafts, especially if the shafts are long, as they will be for a three or four-barrel tumbler. It helps to round the shoulder at the end of the shaft with a file and to soap the shaft liberally with water and detergent before trying to fit the rubber sleeves.

On the opposite ends of the shafts from the drive sheave are mounted two smaller sheaves of equal diameter, connected by a V belt. This ensures equal rotational speed of each shaft and increases the frictional efficiency of the drive.

When using the sample calculations, remember that every characteristic of the tumbling machine follows from the barrel size (Fig. 5-1).

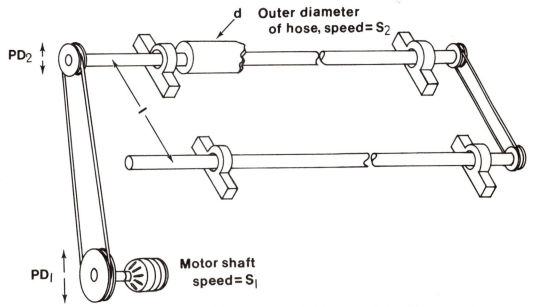

Fig. 5-1 Basic mechanical layout of a typical homemade tumbler.

The diameter of the sheave that fits the main drive shaft may have to be rather large to achieve the desired barrel rotational speed. An alternative would be to use a third shaft or jackshaft for two-step speed reduction. The motor drives this shaft by means of a sheave *one-half the diameter* that would be required in a direct drive. The jackshaft is equipped with a second sheave the same size as that on the motor (for ease of calculation only). This sheave takes a second V belt that drives the main tumbler shaft through a second sheave, also half the diameter of that specified for a direct drive. A jackshaft, however, is usually unnecessary, since sheaves of the diameter needed are readily available at a cost less than that of two smaller sheaves, shaft bearings and additional belt needed for a jackshaft.

Stops

Stops at each end of the tumbler frame keep the barrels centered on the shafts and prevent them from hitting the bearings (Fig. 5-2). In com-

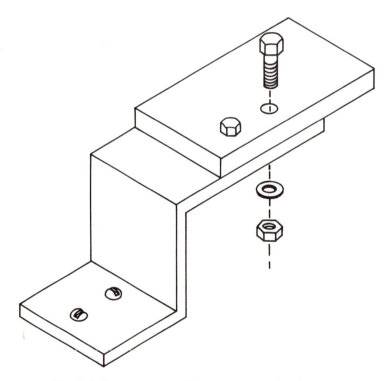

Fig. 5-2 Construction of Masonite stops for the ends of the tumbler barrels.

mercial tumblers these are usually pieces of plastic that ride against the tumbler lid. We have found that a small piece of oil-impregnated Masonite lasts much longer with steel barrels. Stops for all-rubber barrels should be free-turning rollers to prevent damage to the barrel. A small ball-type castor (Fig. 5-3) makes a good frictionless stop.

Building Your Own Tumbler

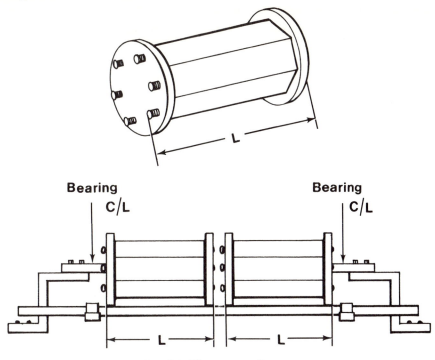

Fig. 5-3 Placement of stops.

TUMBLER DESIGN: SAMPLE CALCULATIONS

Sample calculations which follow will require or determine the following:

- D = Effective barrel diameter
- D_1 = Flange diameter of steel shells (if applicable) or outside diameter of all-rubber (steel, etc.) barrels having no flanges
- L = Overall barrel length (including wing nuts, cover lid, gaskets, lid mount bolts, etc.)
- PD_1 = Motor pulley diameter
- PD_2 = Drive shaft pulley diameter
- d = Diameter of drive shaft (outside diameter of hose covering drive shaft)
- S_1 = Motor running speed
- S_2 = Drive shaft speed
- l = Center-to-center distance between drive shafts
- S = Barrel rotation speed

If the barrels are purchased, the dimensions of the barrel will determine the other unknowns listed. In any case, the barrels are purchased or constructed first; calculations can then be made to determine required sizes of all other parts.

Table 1
Tumbler Operating Speeds as a Function of Effective Barrel Diameter*

Internal Diameter of Barrel (Inches) or Effective Barrel Diameter (Average Dimension Internally for Shapes Other Than Round)	Operating Speed Based on Internal Shape (rpm)			
	Round	12-Sided Internally	Octagonal	Hexagonal
4	48–51	42–47	33–36	26–28
5	45–48	40–44	31–34	23–26
6	41–46	38–42	29–32	22–24
7	39–41	36–40	27–30	20–23
8	36–39	33–36	25–28	19–21
9	34–37	30–33	23–26	18–20
10	32–35	28–31	21–24	17–18
12	29–31	24–27	18–21	16–17
14	26–29	20–24	17–20	15–16
16	25–27	18–22	16–19	14–15
18	24–26	17–20	15–17	13–14
20	23–25	16–19	14–16	12–13
22	22–24	15–18	13–15	11–12
24	21–23	14–17	12–14	10–11

*For coarse grinding in rubber-lined or all-rubber barrels.

Note: If tumbler speed cannot be reduced by 25% for subsequent prepolish and polish cycles, additives must be used to control slurry viscosity after coarse grind.

Metric Equivalents: Multiply number of inches by 25.4 to get millimeters; multiply number of inches by 2.54 to get centimeters.

Tumbler Speed (rpm)

1. Refer to Table 1
2. Diameter of barrel (*effective diameter*) is the average inside diameter (ID) of the liner
3. If the barrel ID is round, refer directly to the table
4. If the barrel is not round, use the following method to determine the mean or average ID (effective barrel diameter = D)

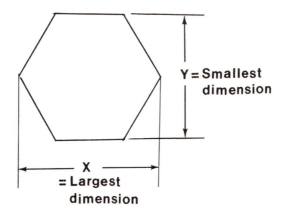

Building Your Own Tumbler

$$D = \text{effective barrel diameter} = Y + \frac{X - Y}{2}$$

EXAMPLE

If: $X = 7\frac{1}{2}''$ and $Y = 6\frac{1}{2}''$

then $D = Y + \dfrac{X - Y}{2}$

becomes $D = 6\frac{1}{2} + \dfrac{7\frac{1}{2} - 6\frac{1}{2}}{2}$

$D = 7''$

We calculated 7" to be the effective barrel diameter for the hexagonal barrel, in this example, and a check of Table 1 shows the speed at which the barrel must rotate to be from 20–23 rpm.

5. Flanged barrel: suppose the barrel liner, in the previous example, fits a steel shell having a flange diameter of 9" (228.6 mm)

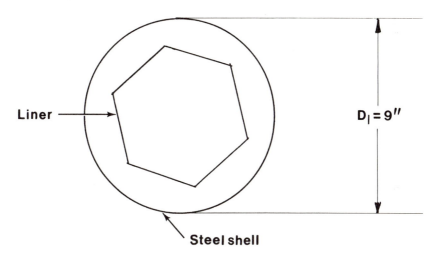

The rotational speed of the flange must be equal to that of the liner or 20–23 rpm.

Drive Shaft Speed

1. Measure the diameter of the flange, or the outside diameter of an all-rubber barrel, and call this dimension D
2. Measure the outside diameter of the radiator hose used to cover the drive shafts and call this dimension d
3. The barrel rotation speed is known from the previous example, and we shall call this speed S. We know $S = 20\text{–}23$ rpm
4. To determine S_2, the drive shaft speed range: $S_2 = S \times \dfrac{D_1}{1.25}$

EXAMPLE

S = Barrel rotation speed = 20–23 rpm

For S = 20 rpm

$$S_2 = 20 \times \frac{9}{1.25}$$
$$= 20 \times 7.20$$
$$= 144 \text{ rpm}$$

For S = 23 rpm

$$S_2 = 23 \times \frac{9}{1.25}$$
$$= 165.6 \text{ rpm}$$
$$= 166 \text{ rpm (approximate)}$$

Therefore we need a drive shaft speed in the range of 144 to 166 rpm to obtain the proper barrel speed in the range of 20–23 rpm.

Selection of Pulleys (PD_1 and PD_2)

1. Approximately $1/16$–$1/20$ hp. (.047–.037 kw) is required for each 10-pound (4.5 kg) tumbler to be run on a machine. Suppose we are constructing a machine for two 10 to 12-pound capacity barrels. A ¼-hp (1.86 kw) motor should be used in this case since ⅛-hp (.093 kw), plus, is required to rotate the two barrels and additional power will be necessary to overcome friction losses in the bearings, drive belts, etc.
2. Assume the motor operating speed is 1750 rpm (conventional speed rating for most ¼ hp × 1800 rpm motors)
3. We have calculated drive shaft speed to be in the range (144 to 166 rpm)
4. The following simple relationship is used to determine motor pulley diameter (PD_1) and drive shaft pulley diameter (PD_2)
   rpm × diameter = rpm × diameter
   S_1 = motor speed = 1750 rpm
   S_2 = drive shaft speed = 144 to 166 rpm
   PD_1 = Motor pulley diameter = 1½″ (assumed); do not use less than 1¼″
   PD_2 = Unknown

FOR LOW SHAFT SPEED: S_2 = 144 RPM

$$PD_2 = \frac{PD_1 \times S_1}{S_2}$$
$$PD_2 = \frac{1.5 \times 1750}{144}$$
$$PD_2 = 18.23''$$
or approximately 18″

Building Your Own Tumbler

FOR HIGH SHAFT SPEED: $S_2 = 166$ RPM

$$PD_2 = \frac{PD_1 \times S_1}{S_2}$$
$$PD_2 = \frac{1.5 \times 1750}{166}$$
$$PD_2 = 15.81$$
or approximately 16"

Therefore if a 1½" (38.1 mm) pulley is used on the motor, then a 16"–18" (406.4–457.2 mm) pulley is required on the drive shaft to provide a proper operating speed range for the tumbler barrels.

5. If the motor pulley dimension is 1¼" (31.75 mm) the resultant drive shaft pulley size would range from 13" to 16" (330.2–406.4 mm)

Distance Between Pulleys; Belt Length Required

1. Assume that we use the 1¼" (31.75 mm) pulley for the motor and a 14" (355.6 mm) pulley for the drive shaft. The center-to-center distance between pulleys should *not be less than* the diameter of the largest pulley. Therefore let's assume that our center distance between pulleys will be roughly 16" (which is greater than the 14" drive shaft pulley diameter)

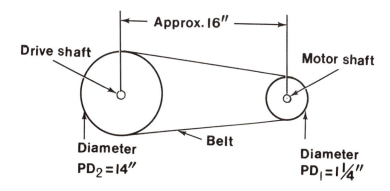

2. Belt length is determined by using the following formula
$$\text{length of belt} = 2C + 1.57(PD_1 + PD_2) + \frac{(PD_2 - PD_1)^2}{4C}$$
Where C = center-to-center distance between drive shafts,
C = approximately 16" for this example
PD_1 = smaller pulley diameter, 1¼"
PD_2 = larger pulley diameter, 14"

$$\text{Length of belt} = 2 \times 16 + 1.57 + (1\tfrac{1}{4} + 14) + \left(\frac{14 - 1\tfrac{1}{4}}{4 \times 16}\right)^2$$

$$= 32 + 1.57 + (15.25) + \left(\frac{12.75}{64}\right)^2$$

$$= 32 + 16.82 + \frac{162.56}{64}$$

$$= 32 + 16.82 + 2.54$$

$$= 51.36$$

Length of belt = 51″ approximately

Since the center-to-center distance will increase with a longer belt, and since the center-to-center distance should be greater than the diameter of the large pulley, a belt length of 51″ or more (not less) is required.

Distance Between Drive Shafts

1. Drive shaft center-to-center distance should be from ½ to ⅝ the outside diameter of the barrel or flange (as case may be) or ½ to ⅝ of PD_2
2. It is wise to have a positive drive between drive shafts when two or more barrels will be run on a single machine. Use pulleys of equal diameter, and determine a belt length (one which is commercially available), which will provide the center-to-center distance between shafts in the proper ½ to ⅝ range
3. If we use, for example, two 1½″ pulleys:

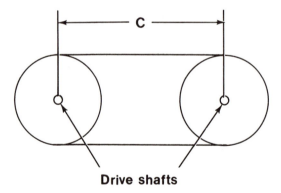

Drive shafts

Both pulleys are same size (1½) = PD_1 = PD_2. Therefore formula for belt length is:

Belt length = $2C + 1.57 + (2PD_2)$
C = ½ to ⅝ of barrel diameter (PD_2)
Since barrel diameter PD_2, is known and equals 9″
   Then: C = ½ (9) = 4.5″ ⎫ Approximate average
   and up to C = ⅝ (9″) = 5.6″ ⎬ is 5″

Building Your Own Tumbler

For C = 5"
Belt length = 2C + 1.57 + (PD$_2$ + PD$_1$)
           = 2C + 1.57 + (1½ + 1½)
           = 2 × (5) + 1.57 + (3)
           = 10 + 4.57 = 14.57
           = 15" approximately
               (a 16" belt would also be satisfactory)

4. If two 2" pulleys were used, the belt length would work out to 16.28" and a 16" belt would be most appropriate

Center-to-Center Distance of Drive Shaft Bearings

We use the following formula to determine the distance between the bearings on a single drive shaft.

Center-to-center Distance = K (L) + 4"
Where L = Total barrel length (with lid on, and taking length of lid bolts etc. into account)
       K = Maximum number of barrels to be run on machine

This will allow enough room for oiled stops or end guides to keep barrels from touching bearings.

Table 2
Suggested Shaft Diameters

Capacity of Single Barrel (pounds)	Minimum Recommended Shaft Diameters* in Inches			
	1	2	3	4
6	¼	¼	⅜	⅜
12	¼	⅜	½	⅝
18	⅜	½	¾	⅞
25	½	⅝	¾	1
50	½	¾	⅞	1

*For one to four barrels supported by two shafts with bearings only at both ends; solid steel shafting assumed.

Metric Equivalents: Multiply number of pounds by .45 to get kilograms; multiply number of inches by 25.4 to get millimeters.

Chapter 6

Vibrating Tumblers

A relatively new type of tumbling unit is now available to the hobbyist, in addition to the standard rotary tumbler. Strictly speaking, it is not a tumbler at all, since the rock container remains fixed, but it is known in the trade as a vibrating tumbler.

TYPES

These machines consist of a container, generally from 4 to 25-pound (1.8–11.25 kg) capacity, mounted on a vibrating plate. The vibration is usually provided by an electric motor. The motor is located beneath the unit. The plate on which the barrel is mounted rests on four heavy springs which separate the plate from the base. The motor mounted on the base has a double-ended shaft with a small pulley on each end. Drive belts from each of these pulleys are connected to a second shaft having eccentric weights at each end. This shaft runs in bearings fixed to the plate beneath the barrel and provides the actual vibration, which can be made more or less severe by changing the angular position of the weights (Fig. 6-3). In the machine used in our tests, there were two weights on each end of the shaft, one fixed and one whose position could be changed to change the tumbling action.

In some units the vibration is electronic, that is, caused by the oscillation of a metal armature in an electric field, as in a fish tank aerator or a vibrating sander.

Vibrating Tumblers

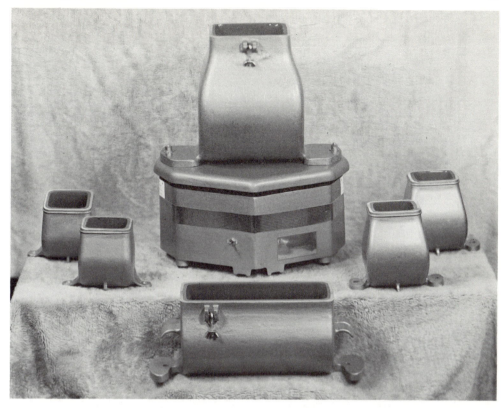

Fig. 6-1 The basic Vibrasonic unit, in which all hoppers are interchangeable. (Geode Industries, Inc.)

Fig. 6-2 The basic Vibratory tumbler with 6-pound (2.7-kg) barrels. (Geode Industries, Inc.)

Fig. 6-3a   Fig. 6-3b

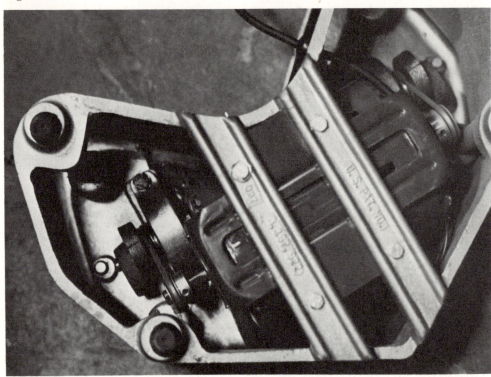

Fig. 6-3c

Fig. 6-3 (a) Shaft arrangement under the base lid of the Vibrasonic tumbler, showing position of the weight on the end shaft. (b) Method of adjusting tumbler vibration by changing the position of the weight on the end of the shaft. (c) Motor with double-ended shaft; belts travel upward to shafts holding weights that generate vibration.

Fig. 1 Typical tumble-polished stones and slabs, including mounted stones.

Fig. 2 Results of using a red hematite polish on a feldspar material such as amazonite.

Fig. 3 Ring designs using wrapped stones.

Fig. 4 Tumble-polished slab used as a clock face.

Fig. 5 Tumbled slab of Botswana agate captured in sterling silver strip. Raised sections are filed off to give scalloped effect to ring.

Fig. 6 Pendants of stones set in Lucite. On right, flowers of garnets, sapphires and diamonds; on left, garnets, diamonds and emeralds. (Courtesy of Sid Meyers, Clearly Stoned, Inc.; designs copyrighted)

Fig. 7 Brooch of electroformed gold on silver with agate slab and freshwater pearls, by Stanley Lechtzin. (Courtesy of Helen Drutt Gallery; photograph by Photo Associates, Philadelphia)

Fig. 8 Choker of agate slab and amethyst crystals in electroformed copper, silver and gold, by Eleanor Moty. (Courtesy of Helen Drutt Gallery; photograph by Photo Associates, Philadelphia)

Fig. 9   Agate pendant made by braiding silver wire.

Fig. 10   Moss agate in a sheet metal setting, designed to follow contours of the stone.

Fig. 11   The base material in this piece of tiger-eye rough is clean and free of fractures.

Fig. 12   Fractured surface of Brazilian agate shows good integrity, cleanliness, color and banding.

Vibrating Tumblers

The vibration of the container can be adjusted so that the stones (but not the tumbler) move in a circular path, continually oscillating against each other and the abrasives in the tumbling solution at about 3000 cycles per minute. Grinding and polishing action occurs much faster than in a rotating tumbler. The entire bath in a vibratory tumbler is in the optimum B layer referred to in Figure 9-1.

We have purchased and tested one of the best of the vibrating tumblers, and found that it lives up to most of the claims made for it, in terms of speed and final polish. It is not the answer to every tumbling problem, however; to get good results with a vibrating tumbler, the hobbyist must exercise the same care in stone selection, cleanliness and loading that we recommend for rotary tumbling. In fact, cleanliness may be even more important (and difficult to achieve).

ADVANTAGES AND DISADVANTAGES

Vibratory tumbling has advantages in addition to its speed. Thin edges have less tendency to chip—although buffering material must be used with both methods—and it removes less material during the roughing stages. This is helpful when tumbling preforms or cabochons, which will retain clean, sharp edges. Some baroques, however, look better with more gently rounded edges. If fact, if the broken rough is extremely jagged, it may be a good idea to run the rock through the rough grind twice or three times. Spalling—lifting of fragments out of the rock face—is also a more severe problem in vibratory tumbling, because of the rapidity of abrasive action.

Because they waste so little material, vibratory tumblers are sometimes used to finish cabochons (domed ovals) of precious materials such as ruby or sapphire. With special dry abrasive compounds, in which the abrasive is contained in inert buffering, medium stones up to 9.5 on the Mohs scale can be tumble polished.

The action of the load can be inspected easily by removing the cover, then running the machine with the top off.

The chief drawback to a vibratory tumbler is its cost. The unit we purchased, with a 14-pound (6.3 kg) container, cost $320 plus shipping costs. Additional barrels cost $80 each; a separate barrel is suggested by the manufacturer for each of four steps. Although it is possible to get by with two barrels, one for the first two grinds and one for the prepolish, the cost of setting up is still substantial.

Much less expensive vibratory tumblers are on the market, but we cannot recommend them for long-term use. By its nature, vibration is a severe test of materials, and any machine designed to withstand it for years of operation is bound to be expensive. A small, 3 to 4 pound (1.4–1.8 kg) capacity tumbler, now available for $85 from Geode Industries with a $9.95 hopper, might be a good compromise (Fig. 6-4).

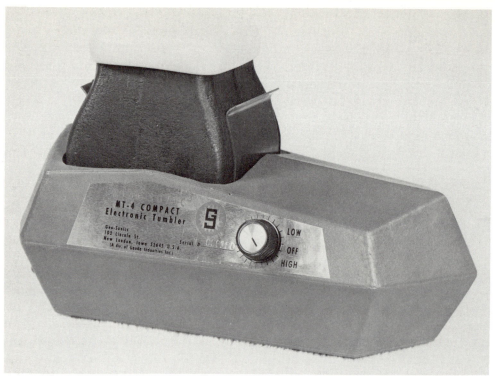

Fig. 6-4a

Fig. 6-4 (a and b) With the increasing popularity of vibratory tumbling, many manufacturers are now producing smaller low-cost models such as those shown. (a) Courtesy of Geode Industries, Inc.; (b) Courtesy of Calway, Inc.

The question to ask is whether the speed of vibratory tumbling is worth the extra expense. If you do not need high production or minimum waste, the rotary tumbler should be perfectly satisfactory. It will provide the same degree of polish and slightly more rounding of the stone surface.

If the hobbyist employs a triple-barrel rotary tumbler, his continuous production, once the first four-step cycle has been completed, will not be much less than what he can achieve with a vibratory unit. As he removes polished stones from one barrel, he will be adding new rough to another.

CHARGING A VIBRATING MODEL

Cleanliness is a prerequisite for all types of tumbling, but is especially difficult to attain with vibratory tumbling. In a vibratory unit the abrasives are in a semi-dry state, a thick "batter" as compared to the thinner slurry suitable to rotary tumbling. When the stones are removed for cleaning and the top is off the container, the batter begins immediately to dry out. It is extremely tenacious, especially if thickened with chemical pellets to control the viscosity.

Some users of vibratory tumblers claim that stones need not be sepa-

Vibrating Tumblers

Fig. 6-4b

rated according to hardness, as they must be for rotary tumbling. This is a fallacy. You can get a polish of sorts with a mixed batch of stones, as you can in a rotary tumbler, but if your objective is a perfect mirror finish, the only way to obtain it is by stone sorting and balancing of sizes as described in Chapters 7 and 8.

Another claim sometimes made is that fewer abrasives are required. The idea is that the coarser abrasives break down as tumbling proceeds, so that a 100 mesh becomes a 320, a 320 becomes a 600 and so on. This is the same principle applied by manufacturers of three-step abrasive kits. It works, but not very well. Abrasives do not break down evenly. Some may still be in the original mesh size while other grains have been pulverized to a powder. The amount of abrasive required is about half of that required in a rotary tumbler of the same capacity.

TUMBLING TIME

When the vibratory tumbler is running it must be inspected regularly, every 8 to 12 hours. This is not only to check the condition of the stones, but also to make sure that the consistency of the slurry is correct, like thick pancake batter. The solution tends to thicken rapidly as it loses moisture; if it becomes too thick the tumbling action is lost.

You will see the entire batch moving around the tumbler fairly rapidly, if the slurry is not too thick. This rotating action should be slower, and the slurry thicker, in the stages after the rough grind. As long as the stones move you will be getting results. As the circular motion slows, the stones are ground less rapidly but are also less subject to breakage and spalling. Tumbling soft materials produces a lot of rock dust that thickens the solution still more. When this happens water must be added until the slurry becomes thin enough for normal tumbling action to resume.

As in rotary tumbling, the time in each step will depend to a great extent on the hardness of the material and its condition upon loading. The rough grind step in a vibrating tumbler may take anywhere from 1 to 6 days, until the surface of each stone is smoothed out and all pits have been removed. Since the abrasive action is so strong, the silicon carbide breaks down in about 12 hours and should be changed every 24 to 36 hours, depending on the size and hardness of the stones in the batch. Large, hard stones wear out the abrasive rapidly.

The second or intermediate grind, if the stones have been rough ground properly, takes from 12 to 24 hours. The tumbling solution should retain its consistency during this period without the addition of water, since less rock dust is being produced. The prepolishing and polishing steps each take from 8 to 24 hours, depending upon the type of material. Hard materials such as agates usually polish faster than soft stones such as Apache Tears or amazonite.

The tumbling instructions in this book apply equally to vibrating and rotating tumblers. The only differences are in the amount of water and abrasive to be added to the batch, the frequency of inspection and the level of the load in the hopper (Fig. 6-5).

If you can use the extra speed of a vibrating tumbler or any of its secondary advantages, by all means spend the extra money on one of the better units. But if you are just beginning the lapidary hobby we recommend the old standby rotary. Purchasing a vibrating unit when you are starting out is like learning to drive in a Rolls-Royce.

It might be a good idea to use the vibratory tumbler for the rough stages, then a rotary tumbler for the prepolish and polish steps. The times required by both machines for these steps are not very different; the rotary tumbler does not require as frequent inspection and produces a better finish. One inspection forgotten during vibratory tumbling may cause the whole batch to be spalled and send you back to step one. If the material is tumbled an extra day in a rotary tumbler, no harm is done.

If Apache Tears or softer materials are to be tumbled, the manufacturer of the vibratory unit recommends Vibradry (manufactured by Geode Industries, Inc.). This is a compound for the final prepolish and polish stages. It comes in grit sizes from 400 to 25,000 (400, 600, 1,200, 2,500,

Vibrating Tumblers

Fig. 6-5 The vibratory tumbler barrel is filled to within an inch or an inch and a half (25.4–38.1 mm) of the top.

8,000, 14,000 and 25,000). Sizes are dictated by the material, softer stones requiring the higher numbers. The harder materials take the lower mesh sizes. Botswana agate, for example, can be final sanded in 400 or 600, prepolished in 2500 and final polished in 14,000 for a very good luster. Apache Tears may be final sanded in 600 or 1200, prepolished in 8000 and final polished in 25,000. Vibradry is used completely dry, thus eliminating the possibility of contamination and the need for extremely close attention to cleanliness of each stone.

The manufacturer of Vibrasonic recommends using a balanced load, meaning an even mixture of small and large pieces. This is often recommended for rotary tumbling as well. We have found, however, that with softer materials, better results are obtained on larger stones when the charge consists of mainly large stones. This results in a more evenly polished stone. The process takes somewhat longer, but the appearance of the finished stone is more desirable. In a vibrator, if a load of harder materials is not balanced (evenly mixed large and small stones), some spalling takes place on the larger pieces, although it is not severe. With obsidians, however, spalling increases substantially when the load is not balanced.

Some things can be done with a vibratory tumbler that are impossible in rotary tumbling. For example, stones set in rings can be polished in dry compounds, together with small stones. And the dry abrasive compounds can also be used to polish very hard materials (above 9 on the Mohs scale) such as garnet, sapphire or ruby.

A TEST

The vibratory tumbler is basically not a new concept, although it is new to the rock and gem business. Manufacturers of vibratory tumblers point out that the process has been used for many years by industrial firms.

Being somewhat skeptical of revolutionary developments in a centuries-old craft, we decided to buy a vibratory tumbler to substantiate or disprove the claim that it is ten times faster than rotary tumbling.

The Vibrasonic unit was received and first tested on fairly hard agate (Botswana) material. We generally tumble this particular agate for about 6 weeks in the rough grind stage to get absolutely perfect stones in the final step. Most of the processing time is taken up in rough grinding. We tumbled the agate for 6 weeks in a rotary tumbler as a control in the experiment.

The Vibrasonic tumbler was capable of rough grinding the stones in slightly less than a week (5 days) using three changes of rough abrasives.

The vibratory tumbler was certainly faster. It remained to be seen whether the final finish would be as good.

The instructions for this type of machine call for two barrels to get an even finish on most regular agates. This seems to be due to the fact that the action is severe enough that sharp points on some materials actually penetrate the plastic liner of the barrel, microscopic particles may break off, or abrasives may impregnate the liner, making it difficult if not impossible to get the barrel completely free of contamination before the next step. This was noticed with subsequent tests on snowflake obsidian. To eliminate contamination, another barrel is necessary.

As we mentioned above, what gives one pause is not that the tumbler needs another barrel, but that the additional barrel costs $80 plus shipping, as compared to about $10 for a rotary tumbler barrel of the same capacity.

However, considering that the tumbler gives results in about one-sixth the time (not one-tenth, as claimed), this extra cost may be justified in a shop where large quantities of material are required and are normally produced in two triple 12-pound (5.4 kg) barrel units. This 14-pound (6.3 kg) single-barrel machine will turn out the same amount of material as six 12-pound rotary barrels.

The tumbler manufacturer recommends checking the batch every 8 hours or less. This was done, and the first thing noticed was that the consistency of the slurry did not remain constant very long. It had a tendency to thicken rapidly, due to the addition of rock dust at a fast rate into a solution that initially is about 50% water and about 50% abrasive by volume. The amount required is about one ounce (.03 kg) of abrasive for each pound (0.4 kg) of stone, or about 14 ounces (.39 kg) by volume for a full load of stones, and an equal amount of water. In rotary tumbling, the stones are covered with water. In the vibratory tumbler the amount of water is just enough to wet the stones and carry the abrasive. Thus it takes

Vibrating Tumblers

very little breakdown of the abrasive or ground-off stone to thicken the slurry to a point where the stones are moving very slowly. An ounce and a half of water had to be added after the first 12 hours. The water is added very slowly to the batch while the tumbler is operating, until the stones begin to move more freely. When adding water the machine is generally running, and it is fairly easy to see what is happening to the slurry. The thickness of the slurry is very important in vibratory tumbling. Too thin a solution will cause spalling: transfer of vibration from the machine to the stones becomes too violent, almost like a series of impacts against a hard mass. This is probably the most important factor in vibratory tumbling. It is important in rotary tumbling as well, but in a vibrating machine it must be checked periodically without fail. Spalling is shown in Figure 6-6; it is very prevalent in softer or more brittle stones, such as snowflake obsidian. The spalling shown occurred in the vibratory tumbler during the second grind.

In the chapters on rotary tumbling it is emphasized that the barrel must be at least half full at all times or the proper finish will not result. This is just as true of vibratory tumbling. As the size of the load is reduced, the amount of activity in the tumbler is also reduced. The load turns over best when there is more material in the tumbler. Thus it is necessary,

Fig. 6-6 Classic examples of spalling can often be found in a batch of brittle snowflake obsidian, or in softer stones.

especially with softer materials, that two batches be rough ground and combined to provide enough material for the second step.

Since the consistency of the slurry is so much thicker in vibratory than in rotary tumbling, the stones themselves are much more difficult to clean between stages. Prior to the removal of the load, we threw about a half cup of water into the tumbler and let it operate for about 30 seconds before final washing. Don't add too much water, or it will splash out. Add the water as the machine is running; the thick slurry will be vibrated off the stones, making them much easier to clean.

The manufacturer recommends the use of a separate barrel for each and every operation when tumbling difficult materials such as Apache Tears and obsidian. The small time saving in the last two stages is not worth the price of two additional barrels. The only benefit would be to, say, a cabochon manufacturer, where thousands of cabs are being made. The hobbyist would find it difficult enough to justify the expense of a single additional barrel, which *is* required.

Indeed, it may be difficult for the hobbyist to justify the cost of the vibratory tumbler in itself. The average hobbyist may not be able to afford the $300 plus required for the initial setup, although there are some new, smaller and less expensive models on the market, as shown in Figure 6-4.

The only thing one gains is speed. Our test results were identical or even slightly less perfect than those obtained with rotary-tumbled control batches of both agate and obsidian. However, this may have been due to the fact that our familiarity with rotary tumbling procedures was great, while vibratory tumbling was quite new and we had only followed manufacturer's instructions.

Chapter 7

Getting Started—Rough Grind

BREAKING ROUGH

Breaking rock is an extremely important step in tumbling; the stones that you wind up with, after six to eight weeks of attention will be roughly 30% smaller in size and similar in shape to those you started with. The major differences are that they will be polished and the edges will be rounded.

We recommend using a ½-inch (12.7-mm) steel plate resting on a wad of newspapers as an anvil for breaking the rock. The padding absorbs shock and prevents the plate from bouncing around on the concrete floor or breaking it up. The hammer can be a mason's pick or a cracking hammer (similar to a small sledge hammer). There are also rock cleavers on the market that fracture stone by mechanical pressure but an equally good job can be done with a hammer, at lower cost (Fig. 7-1).

You will also need something to put the rocks in, a pair of safety glasses and work gloves since broken edges and splinters of rock can be very sharp.

When breaking up material that fractures conchoidally, the *convex* side of the fracture should be placed against the plate before the piece is struck again with a hammer as shown in Figure 7-2. If the concave side is down, as is the natural tendency, the rock will splinter instead of breaking into the chunky fragments that are best for tumbling. Try to break along natural fractures.

Some rocks need not be broken at all. Apache Tears, beach pebbles and carnelian pebbles should be tumbled as is, no matter what their size.

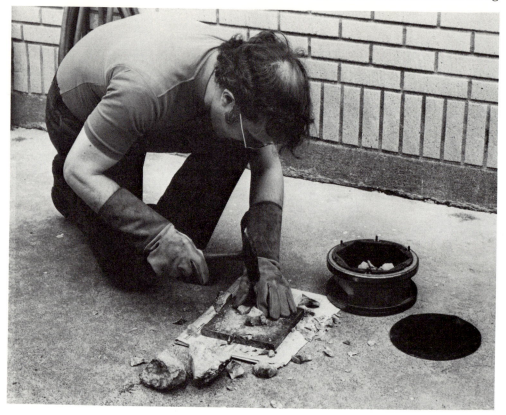

Fig. 7-1 Breaking up rough is a tedious but extremely important step in tumbling.

If the unbroken stones are fairly uniform, without gross irregularities, they should be tumbled in a balanced mix instead of one consisting of all large stones, since the severe rounding and surface removal that occurs in an all-large batch will be unnecessary. A batch of all large Apache Tears will usually develop fine spalling or pitting that results in surface haze and no polish.

The sizes of the broken rock will depend upon the use to which the finished pieces are to be put. Much jewelry is made from small pieces that would fit through a sorting mesh about ⅜-inch (9.5 mm) square. These

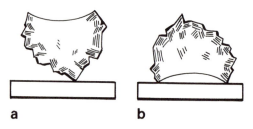

Fig. 7-2 (a) The correct way to break a stone that fractures conchoidally. (b) The wrong way.

Getting Started—Rough Grind

Fig. 7-3 Samples ready for rough grinding. One is a balanced load, the other an even load of large material.

small pieces are useful for rings, bracelets and items made from clusters of small stones. The large pieces are generally used for pendants, bola slides and similar items. When breaking pieces less than an inch (25.4 mm) across, it is wise to go to a smaller size hammer to avoid crushing or powdering the stone.

Figure 7-3 shows two suitable samples from batches of stones ready for rough grinding. One sample is from a *uniform* load, the other from a *balanced* load. A balanced load has a large number of small stones, fewer large ones, and the rest a range of intermediate sizes. An even or uniform mix contains all small or all large stones.

DETERMINING TUMBLING LOADS

There is no advantage to tumbling an entire batch of small stones. If small and large stones are tumbled together, the large stones will usually have more concave surfaces and irregularities, although their polish will not be affected. If all the stones are large, the results will be much more uniform and satisfying in shape, almost like irregularly shaped eggs.

We consider the shapes obtained by tumbling all large stones to be more desirable for use in jewelry, but the use of additives is an absolute necessity when tumbling such a batch. In a balanced load, smaller stones cushion the shock of collision between larger pieces, a role that *must* be filled by additives if all large stones are being tumbled.

A large, even mix will take longer to finish than a balanced mix. There are no small stones to carry abrasive into the crevices or hollows; therefore, much more stone must be ground away before the surface becomes polishable.

As we are breaking up rock, we also look for pitted sections or sponge-like matrix material that must be discarded as unpolishable. Any rock with holes or pits that extend into the base material must be avoided, since it will prevent clean stones from taking a polish.

Chips or slivers are most prominent when breaking up conchoidally fracturing material—obsidian, goldstone or cullet (glass). Crystalline quartz materials such as amethyst or rose quartz also produce large numbers of slivers.

Don't try to tumble the slivers. All that will come of it is smaller, thinner slivers, unusable even if polished. They will only reduce the amount of material that could be produced if all the broken pieces were chunks. The main reason for eliminating slivers is that they are the most likely pieces to break during tumbling and can ruin an otherwise perfect batch. All the shapes should be watched to some extent and controlled as much as possible while breaking the rock. The tumbler isn't going to change the shape extremely. For example, it will not remove a step (a

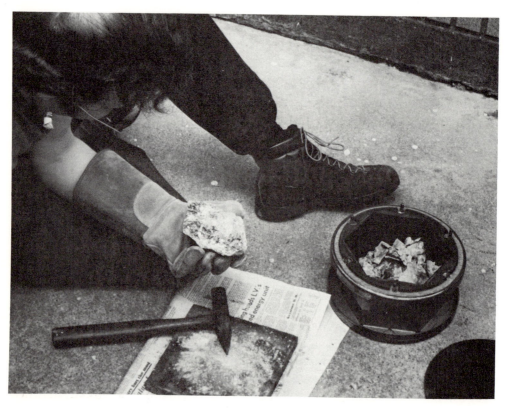

Fig. 7-4 Examine rough material prior to and during breaking to determine which areas will have to be discarded due to porosity or other defects.

Getting Started—Rough Grind

break that occurs often in materials that fracture along cleavage planes, such as feldspar) from the surface. You will find that some pieces of this material look like two cubes joined together. Since they are joined at about a 90°-angle, the defect will not be removed by tumbling and the piece should be broken again to form two small blocks.

Some stones will break up very neatly, but there will always be a certain amount of slivering and rock dust. It will seem that a lot of material is being thrown away (up to 15% or 20% of the load with obsidian) before it even gets to the tumbler. The weight of the end result when tumbling obsidian may be only 40% that of the starting weight. The loss is due to material discarded during sorting after the various steps. The sorted material, of course, can be rebroken if necessary and taken through the rough grind again, as long as it does not have internal fractures or pitting that make it entirely unusable.

During the crushing or breaking operation, rock splinters fly through the air, which is why we recommend safety glasses. Safety glasses will also protect against metal chips that can fly off the hardened face of a hammer.

Some manuals recommend the inclusion of "dust," small sandlike particles left after breaking the rock, in the batch. There is little advantage

Fig. 7-5 Common snowflake obsidian and baby spot obsidian not only look different, but also fracture somewhat differently.

to including these particles. They only serve to thicken the slurry and, in the rough grind, the slurry should be *thinner* than in the subsequent steps.

The percentage of larger chunks—¾ to 1½ inch (19–37 mm) or larger—in a balanced mix should be about 2% to 3% of the load by number, or up to 25% by weight. A balanced mix must be used in a vibrating tumbler (see Chapter 6), although we have achieved good results in these machines with an even mix of large, relatively hard agates.

CHARGING THE TUMBLER

The tumbler should definitely be charged with a single type of rock. We have categorized the various materials according to their ability to be tumbled together. For the purposes of this book, the same type means that they are from the same group, as indicated in Table 3. There are occasions when certain stones from one group can be tumbled with those of a different group. In general, however, we do not suggest any mixing of groups. The best method includes a load completely made up of one type of rock—all amethyst with amethyst, agate with agate. And certain stones *must* be tumbled by themselves; they will not even withstand tumbling with stones of similar hardness. Apache Tears are one example. They are the same basic type of material as obsidian. But the minerals that form the "snowflakes" in snowflake obsidian can abrade the clear surface of the Apache Tears and haze the whole batch.

Abrasives

The amounts of abrasive required for each tumbling step are shown in Tables 4, 5 and 6. When a batch of all large stones is tumbled, the amount of abrasive in each batch can be reduced. However, the rough grind must be repeated two to three times.

A larger amount of abrasive is required in a balanced batch. The recommended amounts, however, should not be exceeded. Too much abrasive defeats the purpose. Less grinding action takes place. Too little, and the abrasive wears out before the step is complete.

As shown in Table 4, we recommend starting out with a 60/90 mesh silicon carbide "wire-saw abrasive." An 80 or 100 mesh would also be acceptable, but specified mesh sizes are more expensive than the 60/90 mesh. Coarser abrasives, 30 or even 25 mesh, could also be used, but then a second rough grind with a 60/90 or 100-mesh grit becomes absolutely necessary before the intermediate grind. The very coarse abrasives are sometimes useful in reducing the contours of hard materials such as Brazilian agate or carnelian pebbles, especially large pieces, in some cases reducing the time of the initial grind by 7 to 9 days.

Getting Started—Rough Grind

Table 3
Compatible Tumbling Materials by Group

Group A: Soft Materials	Group B Soft but Brittle in Nature	Group C: Medium Hard	Group D: Hard Crystalline	Group E: Hard Material	Group F: Material Which Must Be Tumbled Alone	Group G: Very Hard
Malachite	Azurite	Rhodonite	Amethyst	Agates	Apache tears	Beryl
Serpentine	Turquoise†	Olivine	Rose quartz	Carnelian	Obsidian (all varieties)	Spinel
Rhodochrosite	Lazurite	Diopside	Rutillated quartz	Brazilian Lace	Cullet (glass)	Topaz
Varisicite	Lazulite	Pyrite	Citrine	Dendritic	Goldstone	Corundum
Smithsonite	Common opal	(more than 40%)	Smoky quartz	Plume	Coal	Ruby
Malachite/ Azurite	Spars	Jadeite	Rock crystal (quartz)	Moss	Garnet**	Sapphire
Chrysocolla	Amazonite	Zircon	Tourmaline	Sagenite		Emerald
Amber*	Peristorite	Pyrolucite	Aquamarine	Montezuma nodules		
	Moonstone	Prehnite	Tourmalated quartz	Coral— Agatized‡		
	Rhyollite	Sodalite		Beach agates		
	Apatite	Unakite		Tiger eye‡		
	Coal†	Limestone		Epidote		
	Labradorite (mother of pearl)	Howlite		Jasper		
		Psilomelane‡		Petrified wood		
				Petrified bone		
				Zircon‡		
				Fire agate		
				Chalcedony		
				Beryl‡§		
				Topaz‡§		
				Spinel‡§		
				Adventurine		

*Best polished by hand after fine grind (group F material).
†Also a group F material.
‡Possible group F.
§Possible group G.
**Requires approximately 2–3 times more coarse grind and twice all other grinding time.

Table 4
Coarse Grind in 60/90 Wire-Saw Abrasive or 80 Mesh*

Stone Group	Stone Size	Amount of Abrasive (per 10 pounds stone)	Running Time (days)	Comments
A,B	Balanced Load	10–12 oz., ¾ cup 10–12 oz., ¾ cup	5 5–6	First Coarse Grind Second Coarse Grind (generally required)†
A,B	All Large	10–12 oz., ¾ cup 10–12 oz., ¾ cup 8–10 oz., ½ cup	4 4 5	First Coarse Grind Second Coarse Grind Third Coarse Grind (sometimes required)†
C,F	Balanced Load	14–16 oz., 1 cup 10–12 oz., ¾ cup 8–10 oz., ½ cup	5–6 6 7	First Coarse Grind Second Coarse Grind (required) Third Coarse Grind (sometimes required for group F)‡
C	All Large	14–16 oz., 1 cup 10–12 oz., ¾ cup 8–10 oz., ½ cup	4–5 4–5 5–6	First Coarse Grind Second Coarse Grind (required) Third Coarse Grind (sometimes required)†
D,E	Balanced Load	14–16 oz., 1 cup 14–16 oz., 1 cup 10–12 oz., ¾ cup	6–7 7 8	First Coarse Grind Second Coarse Grind Third Coarse Grind (usually required)†
D,E	All Large	14–16 oz., 1 cup 14–16 oz., 1 cup 10–12 oz., ¾ cup 8–10 oz., ½ cup	5 5–6 7 8	First Coarse Grind—Material requiring re-breaking visible at this time (group D) Second Coarse Grind Third Coarse Grind Fourth Coarse Grind (generally required on hard group E)
G	Balanced Load (small)	10–12 oz., ¾ cup For any grind	Total running time may include 6–10 stages. Determine by inspection	Materials Best Handled In Vibratory Tumbling Machines—Frequent sortings required between grinds

*Additives for all stone groups except G are ½ tsp. bicarbonate of soda and ½ tsp. detergent for each batch; for group G, use ½ tsp. of detergent *only* after first stage if no gas increase is noted.
†Examine materials in wet *and dry* condition to make this determination.
‡Group F materials which appear finished after second grind should not be put through third grind, but returned to the second grind (same slurry) for 2–3 additional days of tumbling. This will assure abrasive breakdown necessary to proceed to subsequent fine grinding stage.
Metric Equivalents: Multiply number of ounces by 28 to convert to grams; divide number of cups by 4 to convert to liters.

Getting Started—Rough Grind

Time Requirements

In general we recommend much more rough grinding time than the instructions that come with most tumbling machines. Some hobbyists may be satisfied with the results of 5 to 8 days' rough grind. If the highest quality is desired, however, the material must be rough ground much longer—two, three or four times the period suggested by many tumbler manufacturers. Stones processed in this way will have no surface flaws after polish. Any surface cracks, parallel to or under the surface, will have been removed, whereas they will appear as defects or "blisters" in the polished stones if shortcuts are taken. All indentations or unground portions will also be removed. The gem will be completely devoid of flaws not inherent in the stone itself, which might otherwise remain from the breaking-up process, and 90% of the batch will be usable. (Almost 100% for Apache Tears.)

If the times recommended here are reduced by about 30%, the amount of perfect material will be correspondingly reduced by 30%. In other words, the amount of usable material in the final batch will be reduced by less time in rough grind. By an extra week of grinding, you thus eliminate four or more weeks of additional work in regrinding imperfect stones from the final batch.

Is it worthwhile to spend the extra time, since some of the material will have to be reground anyway? Those who tumble stones as a business find that their labor and the running times of their machines have a definite value. They find it more economical to spend the extra time in rough grind, as recommended in the accompanying tables, and emerge with almost the entire batch in usable form.

A useful test of the value of extra rough grinding is to proceed according to the tumbler manufacturer's directions with one batch of material and follow the directions in this book with another batch. Compare the shape and finish of the cleaned and dried gemstones when the last step has been completed. Mediocre results may be acceptable; the objective of our recommendations is professional results.

Grit sizes for each phase:

Coarse grind—	60/90 wire-saw abrasive (silicon carbide)
Fine grind—	320-mesh silicon carbide
Prepolish—	Tripoli or 600/800-mesh silicon carbide
Polish—	tin oxide (or cerium oxide)

Abrasive mesh sizes are not the most critical aspect of the tumbling procedure. Usually the hobbyist can stock only one mesh size in each grade—rough, intermediate, prepolish or fine, and polish.

Filling the Tumbler

The broken stones are *placed* in the tumbler handful by handful, not dumped or poured in. This is not important in the first grind, but it is wise to get into the habit, as careful handling of the stones becomes more and more important as work progresses. When pouring, the stones strike each other with considerable impact and may easily break.

The tumbler should be filled to half or five-eighths of its capacity. Any larger amount, even three-quarter capacity, will slow the abrasive action. (see Chapter 9). The same is true of loads smaller than those recommended, with the additional hazard of edge cracking.

If the tumbler is not five-eighths full, you may not get enough material out of the rough grind to load the intermediate step properly, especially when tumbling softer materials. This is what makes a two-barrel tumbler so convenient. Two batches can be ground at the same time, thus guaranteeing sufficient material for the next stage. There are two alternatives: rough grind another batch in the same tumbler and combine it with the first or use buffering compounds—wood chips, plastic pellets or rice hulls, to make up the deficiency.

After all rough grinding stages have been completed, the tumbler may be just half full. It is possible to proceed to the next step without filler, but filler media must be added after the intermediate grind to make up for the slight amount of material lost in this step.

The stones are level now in the barrel. The abrasive is added to the stones and shaken down between them. About half a teaspoonful of baking soda is added to prevent gas buildup, plus enough water to raise the water line to almost cover the top layer as shown in Figure 7-6.

ROUGH GRIND

The barrel is then sealed and the machine started. It will make more noise than usual when rough tumbling begins. You will hear the stones clicking inside the barrel. One advantage of a rubber liner is reduction of noise, as well as cushioning the load and improving tumbling action. The rubber also carries the abrasive, unlike a harder material, and is thus not affected by it. The walls of glass jars or metal cans, without liners, would be ground away very quickly.

After the first few days, the noise should have quieted to a swishing and rumbling sound. This is when most of the abrasive action takes place. The stones have been ground somewhat and rock dust has thickened the slurry. For the next four days, abrasive efficiency will decrease slightly as the abrasive breaks down to a finer mesh size.

With a *balanced* mix, the initial coarse grind should take from 5 to 8 days. With an *even* (all large) mix, the initial grind will last about 4 days, since larger stones pulverize the abrasives more quickly. Also, a smaller

Getting Started—Rough Grind 67

Fig. 7-6 Proper water level in the barrel with a batch of preground obsidian.

amount of abrasive is required with the even mix than with the balanced mix. There will be more rough grinding steps with the large stones, but the amount of abrasive in each step will be less, so that the total amount of abrasive required to take a batch through the rough grinding stage will not be much more than that needed for a balanced load (25% to 50% more). Remember, adding more abrasives will not speed up the process and may indeed slow it down.

When you open the tumbler after 4 or 5 days, the slurry will have the consistency of thick cream. Usually the abrasives have broken down and tumbling efficiency has dropped severely for that step. Wash the stones—

you needn't get them completely clean since they are going into the same abrasive again—and recharge the tumbler, after following the sorting procedure described below. If you are not sure that the abrasive is worn out, it may be tested by rubbing the slurry between the thumb and forefinger. If the slurry feels gritty, it has some coarse abrasive quality left.

Most materials do not require more than two rough grinds. The necessity for a third rough grind can be determined by inspection. Will the stones look suitable for your purposes when polished? After the coarse grinding steps, not much more material will be removed, so the shapes you see at this stage will be approximately those of the finished stones. What you see is what you get. Do not rely simply on the amount of time spent in rough grinding: inspect the stones carefully. It is best to wash the batch, let it dry and then look at it. Appearance when wet can be deceptive.

Eventually, you should be able to tell how much rough grinding will be necessary merely by looking at the broken material before it enters the tumbler. As mentioned above, some materials break very cleanly into even, uniform chunks—some types of moss agate with lots of inclusions or "moss" break like this—in which case only a single grind may be neces-

Fig. 7-7 Snowflake obsidian completely rough ground and ready for intermediate grinding.

Getting Started—Rough Grind

sary. Thus, although we recommend two grinds, if inspection of the dry stones shows satisfactory shape and elimination of surface flaws, by all means go to the next step. Further rough grinding will only waste time and material.

SECOND ROUGH GRIND

After the first rough grind is completed, the stones must be sorted. All stones with pitting and primary fracturing must be removed and, if at all usable, treated as if they were freshly broken rough.

At this point, a glance at the flow chart in Figure 7-9 will show how to proceed. The stones are actually being sorted into three categories: (1) those that can go directly into a second coarse grind to improve their surface and shape (Table 4); (2) those which, because of very visible internal fractures or other defects, must be rebroken and included with a subsequent batch of freshly broken rough; (3) those which, because of pitting or other defects are completely unusable and must be discarded. Figure 7-10 shows samples of carnelian to sort out for rebreaking and regrinding.

Fig. 7-8 Many tumbling materials require very close inspection between grinding steps.

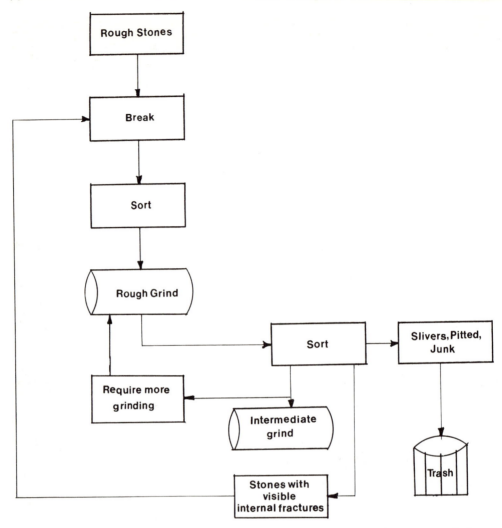

Fig. 7-9 Flow chart shows sequence of steps in sorting and breaking material during coarse grinding stages.

After complete rough grinding, stones are hazy in appearance when dry, although wet stones always look shiny. All rough edges will be rounded off and recesses will be of a uniform consistency with the more rounded surfaces. There will be bulges and dimples, but no area of the stone should appear jagged. Stones which are unfinished may have pits or areas which look like a piece of soft clay into which a fingernail has been pressed. These are moon-shaped depressions typical of a stone which has not been ground enough in the roughing stage.

We have seldom found a single rough grinding step sufficient to give satisfactory results, except perhaps in the case of Apache Tears or beach pebbles. After the first week of the second rough grind the stones must be cleaned up and inspected again.

Getting Started—Rough Grind

Fig. 7-10 Internal fracturing, as seen in this carnelian, is visible after the first rough grind. Fractures should be completed with a small hammer and the fragments retumbled with next run of similar agate through the rough grind.

Refer to Table 4 for second coarse grind and subsequent coarse grinding procedure. By weight, approximately 1 pound (0.4 kg) of coarse 60/90 abrasive is added to each 10 pounds (4.5 kg) of stones, (0.28 kg) for hard materials; for softer materials, about 0.8 pounds (0.28 kg) of abrasive is required for each 10 pounds (4.5 kg) of stones.

Following the rough grinding procedures shown in Table 4 will make it much easier to obtain excellent results in subsequent steps.

Chapter 8

Intermediate Grind, Prepolish and Polish

After the final (second or third) rough grinding, the stones are once again removed from the tumbler and washed *thoroughly*. Any cracked or broken pieces should be taken out at this point. We generally use a plastic collander with holes about 3/32-inch (2.38-mm) square. The sand-sized chips that fall through such a collander can be thrown away, as they will be too small to have any use after the following stages. The tumbler is rinsed out and washed very thoroughly, the stones replaced and the tumbler charged for the intermediate grind. There is really no way of telling, short of experience, when stones have been adequately rough ground except to check surfaces carefully for flaws wet and dry. If they appear in the dry condition to be desirable as far as overall shapes are concerned, and free of defects, the second or intermediate stage can begin.

INTERMEDIATE GRIND

In the intermediate stage the consistency or viscosity of the slurry becomes more important than in rough grinding. It becomes even more critical in the third and fourth stages. To start out with the right amount of ingredients to ensure proper viscosity, it is necessary to put the stones back in the tumbler, after complete washing, at which point the finer, intermediate-mesh abrasive for step two is added; it is then washed down into the stones as water is poured into the batch. A pinch (¼ teaspoon) of

Intermediate Grind, Prepolish and Polish

soap (powered laundry detergent) and an equal amount of bicarbonate of soda are added to prevent gas buildup and the water is added last so that it appears about halfway up the top layer of stones. Remember that the viscosity of the slurry will increase as tumbling progresses.

The tumbler at this point should be *at least* half full. If it is not, it is necessary to go back and tumble more stones through the rough grind so the batch can be brought to the one-half or five-eighths level before proceeding. Cracked or chipped material from the earlier rough grind that has been retumbled the same number of times may be used in this makeup batch. If the material is not cracked all the way through, as may often happen with materials such as rose quartz or amethyst, it should be taken to the cracking block and broken along the fracture line before going back to first rough grind. Some cracking, which shows up as white internal lines in the stone, is unavoidable in most crystalline quartz materials. Thus only those stones that show unsightly fractures after the rough grind need be rebroken. This is a very time-consuming operation, but well worth the effort with such stones as amethysts (Fig. 8-2). This operation may also be necessary with some of the spars, where certain of the stones after rough grinding may show squared-off fractures, like steps.

Follow Table 5 for the intermediate grind. With some materials it may be necessary to begin using buffering materials such as plastic pellets or rice hulls as early as the intermediate grind to prevent spalling and chipping. Apache Tears and the obsidians in general, snowflake obsidian or sheen obsidian, glass or cullet, all must be buffered starting with the second grind. Others need buffering only in the pre-polish and polishing steps.

The clear quartzes, such as amethyst, can also stand some buffering at this point for best results. The buffering compounds are very inexpensive and, if there is any question about the necessity of using them, they should be added to guarantee good results. About 8 ounces (.22 kg) by volume in the intermediate grind is all that is required for the quartzes. Cullet and obsidians require more. Two measuring cups per 10 pounds (4.5 kg) of stones would not be too much. All abrasives and additives such as soap, sugar or bicarbonate of soda should be added before the water. If water is added first, the volume of water in the batch will be too great. If one adds the water first, then the dry materials, the water in a 10-pound batch would rise from 1 to 1½ inches (from 25.4 mm to 38.1 mm) above the stones and the resultant slurry will be too thin for good results. Stones in a thin slurry will collide too violently. Buffering compounds—pellets and wood chips and other materials that do not go into solution—should be added to the batch after the water. Thickeners, such as Tumbletrol or sugar, are used specifically to prevent violent action in the tumbler by increasing the viscosity of the solution. Tumbletrol is a compound in tablet form that when added to water makes it "stringier"; sugar is slightly more expensive but more readily available and will do the same job.

Fig. 8-1a

Fig. 8-1b

Fig. 8-1c

Fig. 8-1d

Fig. 8-1e

Fig. 8-1f

Fig. 8-1g

Fig. 8-1h

Fig. 8-1i

Fig. 8-1j

Fig. 8-1 Sequence used between all steps in tumble polishing: (a) Liner is removed from shell. (b) Stones are carefully poured into the collander. (c) Stones are washed. (d) Barrel is washed thoroughly. (e) All chips and debris are rinsed thoroughly from the inside of the barrel liner. (f) Stones are washed in the collander as a group. (g) Individual handfuls can be given a cursory inspection as they are washed. (h) Stones are placed, not poured, back into the liner. (i) Liner is wiped dry to prevent rusting of steel shell. (j) Abrasives, water and additives are added to the stones. (k) Lip of the liner is wiped with a soap solution to provide the best seal. The tumbler is then sealed and placed on the machine immediately.

Fig. 8-1k

Fig 8-2 Internal fractures in amethyst. Some are severe enough that the stones will have to be rebroken. In others, the internal flaws are not unsightly enough to make it necessary to break them. The stones in this picture have been completely polished so that flaws will show up photographically.

Table 5 shows the required amounts for 10 pounds of stones. For a 3-pound tumbler, simply take 33⅓% and so on. If a cup of material is needed for a 10-pound batch, use a third of a cup for a 3-pound batch.

PREPOLISH TUMBLING

When the intermediate grind is finished, the stones are again *thoroughly washed.* At this point, the thoroughness of the washing gains importance. Check the edges and corners of each stone when dry to see if there is any inconsistency in surface finish between these areas and the flatter portions. Under a magnifying glass of 10X the two surfaces should look identical. You are looking for pits and very tiny spalled sections on the edges as compared to the flats. Spalling shows up as shiny spots where material has actually flaked away from the surface. These are particularly noticeable on obsidian, one of the more difficult materials to polish. If the stones look quite uniform under the magnifying glass, which they should if all the preceding steps have been followed, then it is time to go on to the prepolish stage.

Intermediate Grind, Prepolish and Polish

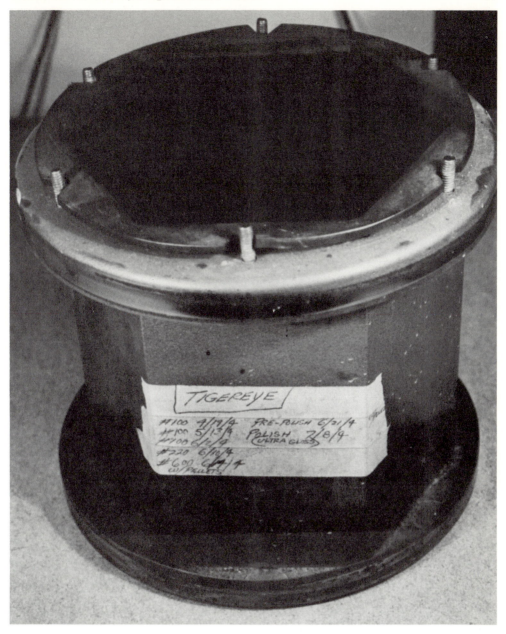

Fig. 8-3 To keep track of the batch being processed, it's a good idea to label the tumbler barrel with its contents for each step.

Table 5 Intermediate or Fine Grind

Stone Group	Stone Size	Running Time (days)*	Abrasive	Amount of Abrasive (per 10 lb. stone)
A	Balanced Load	4	3F, 320 or 400	12–14 oz., 1 cup
A	All Large	4	3F, 320 or 400	10–12 oz., ¾ cup
B	Balanced Load	4–5	3F, 320 or 400	12–14 oz., 1 cup
B	All Large	4	3F, 320 or 400	10–12 oz., ¾ cup
C	Balanced Load	5–6	3F, 320 or 400	12–14 oz., 1 cup
C	All Large	5	3F, 320 or 400	10–12 oz., ¾ cup
D	Balanced Load	6	3F or 320	12–14 oz., 1 cup
D	All Large	5–6	3F or 320	10–12 oz., ¾ cup
E	Balanced Load	6–7	3F or 320	12–14 oz., 1 cup
E	All Large	6	3F or 320	10–12 oz., ¾ cup
F	Balanced Load	7	400	8–10 oz., ¾ cup
F	All Large		Tumble Materials in Group F as Balanced Load Only	
G		Very Hard Materials Should Be Tumbled in Vibratory Machines (Rotary Tumbling Can Be Used by Running Material Through E Group Process Two Times)		

*Running time can be determined by "forced buffing" on a hard felt machine-run wheel with cerium oxide. If 2–3 seconds of buffing produces a semigloss, proceed with prepolish.

Table 5 Intermediate or Fine Grind, cont'd.

Additives	Comments
¼ tsp. bicarbonate, ½ tsp. detergent, pellets or media to bring load to ½ full	
	600 mesh abrasive can be used but increase running time by 2 days.
¼ tsp. bicarbonate, ½ tsp. detergent, pellets or media to bring load to ½ full	
¼ tsp. bicarbonate, ½ tsp. detergent, bring load to ⅝ level with pellets or other filler	600 mesh abrasive can be used but increase running time by 2 days.
¼ tsp. bicarbonate, ½ tsp. detergent	Increase running time by 1 day if 400 mesh abrasive is used.
¼ tsp. bicarbonate, ½ tsp. detergent	
¼ tsp. bicarbonate, ½ tsp. detergent, pellets or other media	Pellets or other media, such as hardwood chips, rice hulls, etc., should be used to bring load to ½–⅝ level.
¼ tsp. bicarbonate, ½ tsp. detergent, pellets or other media	Pellets or other media, such as hardwood chips, rice hulls, etc., should be used to bring load to ½–⅝ level. (Media is a must for even-sized load.)
¼ tsp. bicarbonate, ½ tsp. detergent	
¼ tsp. bicarbonate, ½ tsp. detergent, add media to bring load to ½ level	If load is at ½ level, add 1 cup media to assure even grinding of "hollow" areas in stones.
¼ tsp. bicarbonate, ½ tsp. detergent, 1 cup pellets or hardwood chips, ½ cup sugar	3F or 320 mesh abrasives can be used, but running time must be increased to 8 days.
Tumble Materials in Group F as Balanced Load Only	
Very Hard Materials Should Be Tumbled in Vibratory Machines (Rotary Tumbling Can Be Used by Running Material Through E Group Process Two Times)	

Metric Equivalents: Multiply number of ounces by 28 to convert to grams; divide number of cups by 4 to convert to liters; multiply number of teaspoons by 5 to convert to milliliters.

Fig. 8-4 Apache Tears, normally considered a difficult material to tumble, can be finished perfectly if proper additives are used.

The stones must be absolutely clean and the buffering compounds should be discarded or saved for subsequent intermediate batches. Tumbletrol or sugar (which we recommend in addition to buffering compounds such as plastic pellets) wash away easily. The compounds, on the other hand, must generally be removed from the batch by panning. Several handfuls of stones are placed in a shallow pan. The pan is rocked back and forth as water runs in one end and over the lip at the other end as shown in Figure 8-7. The lighter pellets spill over the rim of the pan, leaving the heavier cleaned stones behind. This is the easiest way we have found to separate stones from pellets and wood chips. These materials are supposed to float to the surface, but there are always some that become waterlogged, and panning is the only way to remove them. A single abrasive-impregnated pellet can spoil the finish in the next grind. Intermediate-grind abrasives are many times coarser than those used in the prepolish and polish steps; it is imperative that any materials that may carry a single grain of them into the next stages be removed. If buffering compounds are saved, they should be placed in a labelled container noting the stage in which they were used and the abrasive size and should be reused *only* in that stage.

The tumbler is recharged for the third grind, or prepolish, the same way as for the second grind. You will notice in Table 6 that the amount as well as the composition of the additives has changed slightly. The amount

Intermediate Grind, Prepolish and Polish

Fig. 8-5 Level of stones at the end of intermediate grind may have fallen noticeably below the necessary half-full mark, as indicated by the chalk line on the tumbler liner. More material, which has gone through the same number of steps, can be added or filler medium will bring the level up to the proper mark.

82   The Complete Book of Rock Tumbling

Fig. 8-6 Stones and buffering pellets at the end of the prepolish stage.

Fig. 8-7 Removing plastic pellet medium from the tumbled stones by panning.

Intermediate Grind, Prepolish and Polish

of buffering compounds, for example, is somewhat larger. The amount of Tumbletrol or sugar is also increased. What we are doing is thickening the batch still further, while adding to the amounts of buffering materials to compensate for the small amount of stone lost in the intermediate grind and also to make sure that we don't compound any slight fracturing or edge chipping that may have taken place. This type of damage must be kept to an absolute minimum. Thus it is more necessary to add both viscosity (sugar) and cushioning (pellets or wood chips) in the latter stages of tumbling.

The time in the prepolish stage will be seen to be about the same as the time required for intermediate grind. Clean and inspect the stones the same way you did after the intermediate grind. At this point it can be seen quite definitely whether the stones are ready to polish or not.

If previous steps have been followed carefully, the main question now is whether the stones have been left in the prepolish stage long enough. If a leather or felt buff is available, it is a simple matter to detemine if you are ready to polish (Fig. 8-8). The stone is simply buffed for a few seconds with cerium oxide, tin oxide or any other final stage polish (see Table 7). If a mirror finish is readily obtained (Fig. 8-9), the stones are ready for the final step.

POLISH CYCLE

Polishing generally takes only 3 or 4 days, if the batch has been properly prepared. Surprisingly enough, the softer stones—amazonite, spars and so on—require longer to polish than harder materials.

Prior to polish, the stones must be free of all residue and the buffering compounds discarded or placed in labelled containers if they are to be saved.

If a buffing wheel is not available, check the surface for pits, spalling, or uneven finish with a magnifying glass.

Recharge the tumbler as for previous grinds, adding the dry compounds first, except for buffering materials, then the water. Stop pouring immediately when you see the water rising between the stones. Then pour very gradually until the water comes about halfway up but does not cover the top layer of stones. If this level is exceeded, the entire solution—water, Tumbletrol or sugar, and abrasive—will have to be emptied out and the process begun all over again.

Bicarbonate of soda can be omitted. The other additives are shown in Table 7. Soap is important in both the polish and the prepolish stages. It helps to clean off the residue of prepolish and also acts to reduce surface tension of the water to allow complete contact between the polish and the stone. It acts as a thickening agent, and in the polish step it may also serve as a burnishing agent to help polish the stones.

Table 6 Prepolish

Stone Group	Stone Size	Running Time (days)	Abrasive	Amount of Abrasive (per 10 lb. stone)
A	Balanced Load	5	Standard Prepolishes, Tripoli, #800 Mesh	10–12 oz., 1 cup
	All Large	5	Standard, Tripoli, #800 Mesh	8–10 oz., ¾ cup
B	Balanced Load	5	Standard, Tripoli, #800 Mesh	10–12 oz., 1 cup
	All Large	5	Standard, Tripoli, #800 Mesh	8–10 oz., ¾ cup
C	Balanced Load	6	Same or #600 Mesh	10–12 oz., 1 cup
	All Large		Same or #600 Mesh	8–10 oz., ¾ cup
D	Balanced Load	Prepolish 5 days; #600 7 days	Standard Prepolishes or #600 Mesh	Standard = 1 cup #600 Mesh = ¾ cup
	All Large*	Prepolish 5 days; #600 7 days	Standard Prepolishes or #600 Mesh	Same as for balanced load
E	Balanced Load	7	Standard Prepolishes or #600 Mesh	Same as group D, balanced load
	All Large	6	Standard Prepolishes or #600 Mesh	Same as group D, balanced load
F	Balanced Load	6	Standard Prepolishes or #600 Mesh	Standard = ¾–1 cup #600 = 4–5 oz., ⅓ cup
	All Large		Tumble Group F Materials in Balanced Load Only	
G			Very Hard Materials Are Best Handled in Vibratory Machines Using Vibra-Dry or Other Similar Dry Media	

*Recommend using a balanced load for group D types; otherwise thickener should be added.

Table 6 Prepolish, cont'd.

Additives	Comments
¼ tsp. bicarbonate, ¼ tsp. detergent, 1–1½ cups pellets or other media	#600 mesh can be used if only 6–8 oz. are used and running time is increased to 6–7 days (determine by buff test)
Use enough pellets with above additives to bring load to ⅝ full	Same as for balanced load.
See group A	Same as group A, balanced load.
See group A, all large load	
See group A	If #600 mesh is used with group C stones, decrease amounts by 25%.
See group A, all large load	
Same as group A, all large load	Use more pellets or other filler on translucent stone types (up to ⅝ to ¾ full level for all large).
Same as group A, all large load—up to ¾ full with media	Use 1 cup sugar as additional additive for translucent types.
Same as group A, balanced load	Pellets not required if load is already to ⅝ level.
Same as group A, all large load	
Same as group D, with enough sugar to thicken slurry & pellets to bring level to ⅝ to ¾	Mix sugar (or thickening tablets) with water and then add to stones to get syrupy slurry.

Tumble Group F Materials in Balanced Load Only

Very Hard Materials Are Best Handled in Vibratory Machines Using Vibra-Dry or Other Similar Dry Media

Metric Equivalents: Multiply number of ounces by 28 to convert to grams; divide number of cups by 4 to convert to liters; multiply number of teaspoons by 5 to convert to milliliters.

Fig. 8-8 Stones can be test polished on a buffing wheel. This will determine if prepolish cycle is complete.

Fig. 8-9 After a few seconds on the buffing wheel, a polish should begin to appear on the stone if prepolish is complete.

Intermediate Grind, Prepolish and Polish

The most important step before polishing is complete inspection of the batch. All cracked and chipped pieces, no matter how small, must be removed. This takes some time, but it is imperative for a good polish, since these small pieces act almost as if they were rough grit. You can waste all the labor and time up to this point if you do not take the 10 or 20 minutes required to go through 10 pounds (4.5 kg) of stones and remove *all* the bad pieces. This can be done conveniently when panning out the pellets, with the stones spread out on the bottom of the pan.

Any stones with spalling, serious internal fractures or pits should also be taken out. Pitted stones may trap abrasive from a previous stage, even after careful cleaning, and release it during the polish stage.

Stones can be checked for polish after tumbling for 2 days. They will generally not be finished, but at this point one can tell if they will require another 1, 2 or 3 days to complete.

Polished stones should look exactly the same when wet or dry. They should have a high, lustrous finish on all areas. If this is not the case, the cause is usually contamination with abrasive from a previous step. But assuming that this is not the case, and all the previous steps were followed carefully, what else may be wrong?

One of the most common defects is polished flat surfaces and unpolished edges. There may be minor spalling of the edges, or they may look as if they were finely sanded in comparison with the glossy surface at the center of the stone. A primary cause of this defect is barrels that were not at least half full during the prepolish and polish operations. This alters the action of the stones in the tumbler. The stones have a tendency to fall further as they climb the wall and drop off, and the sharper edges become chipped. Another reason for lack of finish may simply be bad polishing compound. We recommend tin oxide, although it is more expensive than most other compounds.

After polishing has been completed the stones should be washed once again. If the dry stones are bright enough as is, without a residue of polish, the contents of the washing collander can be emptied gently onto a wad of newspapers, spread out and allowed to dry overnight.

BURNISHING

Softer stones, such as the spars, could go through another operation after the polish. This is called *burnishing*. The stones are washed, replaced in the tumbler, and about one cup of soap flakes added for each 4 pounds (1.8 kg) of stones, plus ¼ cup of sugar or one Tumbletrol tablet. Water is added to just below the level of the batch, and it is tumbled for another 24 hours. This accomplishes two things: it completely cleans the stones and it burnishes them. This step should not generally be necessary. It is helpful, however, if one of the red polishes has been used. These materials can collect in the most minute cracks, making the stone un-

Table 7
Polish

Stone Group	Stone Size	Polish	Amount of Polish	Additives	Running Time (days)	Comments
A	Balanced Load	Tin Oxide	6–8 oz., ½ cup	½ cup soap, 1 cup sugar, pellets or wood chips to bring load level to ⅝ full	4–5 (inspect every 24 hours)	A.F.T. is Air Float Tripoli. Reduce speed of rotation by 30% for round barrels if possible or thicken slurry with sugar or "tumble tablets."
		A.F.T., Cerium Oxide, Chrome Oxide, etc.	12–14 oz., 1 cup			
	All Large	Tin Oxide	6 oz., ⅓ cup	⅓ cup soap, 1½ cups sugar, pellets or wood chips to bring load to ⅝ full	4–5 (inspect every 24 hours)	
		Others (as above)	12 oz., ¾ cup			
B		Same Procedure as Group A, But Increase Sugar or Thickeners by 50%				
C, E*	Balanced Load	Tin Oxide	8 oz., ½ cup	1 cup soap, 1½ cups sugar, pellets to bring load to ½–⅝ level	3–4 (inspect daily)	Inspect carefully all materials of granular nature for undercutting by overpolish.
		Other Polishes	12–14 oz., 1 cup			
	All Large	Tin Oxide	6 oz., ⅓ cup	Same as above, but use 2 cups sugar	3–4 (inspect daily)	
		Others (as above)	12 oz., ¾ cup			
D, F*	Balanced Load	Tin Oxide	8 oz., ½ cup	1 cup soap, 2 cups sugar (or more), media to bring load to ⅝–¾ level	Inspect daily for polish after initial 36 hours	Mix sugar or tablets, and water, until a syrupy mix is obtained. Add to rock, polish, and soap in barrel—then add pellets.
		Others (as above)	12–14 oz., 1 cup			
		Red Hematite (F group)†	10–12 oz., ¾ cup			
	All Large	Tin Oxide	6 oz., ⅓ cup			
		Others	12 oz., ¾ cup			
		Red Hematite (F group)	10 oz., ¾ cup			
G		Very Hard Materials Are Best Handled for Polish in Vibratory Machines, Using "Vibra-Dry," or Other Similar Tumbling Media Having Been Impregnated with Polish				

*Groups are listed together to show procedure only—don't polish materials from D and F groups together.
†Red hematite polishes can be used on other groups, but can be seen in internal stone flaws after polish. Homogeneous materials (group F) can be polished well with the hematite (red) polish.
Metric Equivalents: Multiply number of ounces by 28 to convert to grams; divide number of cups by 4 to convert to liters.

Intermediate Grind, Prepolish and Polish

sightly unless it is completely removed (see color section). It may also be necessary with stones such as moss agate, where the inclusions (the moss) come to the surface and accumulate polishing compounds. You may have to go through the burnishing step twice with such stones. Red polishes should be avoided on moss agates, rutilated quartz, sagonite agate, and any other stones with inclusions. Lace agate has harder and softer bands, and red polishing compounds should not be used on this material for the same reason. Stones with pronounced cleavage planes, such as the feldspars, will become permanently marked by a red polishing rouge, and even repeated soap burnishing will not remove the red veining effect.

You can avoid the problem entirely by using titanium oxide, tin oxide or some other white polishing compound. Others are skin-toned in color and do not appreciably affect the appearance of the stone. The red polishes do work very well on obsidians or on cullet.

Handling of the stones after polishing is also important, to avoid chipping. Tumbling is actually more gentle to the stones than subsequent handling. They should be placed gently in containers, preferably clear plastic, until they are needed for setting in jewelry or other uses. Handle them as little as possible to avoid fingerprints or contamination with oil from the skin, which can adversely affect the bond if the stones are to be set with epoxy resins.

Chapter 9

What's Going on in There?

EFFECTS OF BARREL SHAPE

The effects of round and hexagonal barrel shapes are described in Chapter 4. Hexagonal or octagonal barrels, because their flat sides give the stones an extra "flip" as they change direction rapidly, operate at slower speeds than cylindrical barrels to avoid damaging sensitive materials. It may appear that the more intense action in the hexagonal barrel provides faster rough grinding, but this is not true. Hexagonal barrels require about 40% more time to rough grind.

So why use a hexagonal barrel? Why not use a round barrel and decrease tumbling time? Hexagonal barrels must be run at slower speeds. The slower rotation necessitates longer coarse grinding time, but the barrel speed need not be reduced for prepolish and polish stages of the process. Tumbler manufacturers use the hexagonal shape, which allows the use of a single-speed drive system. The speed selected is appropriate for the finish grinds and coarse grinding will require extra time.

TUMBLING SPEEDS

Speed of rotation is extremely important to good results in tumbling. The basic speed is determined by the size of the barrel. The larger the diameter, the slower the rotation (see Table 1).

The critical speed for tumbling falls within a relatively narrow range.

What's Going on in There?

The stones are carried up the wall of the barrel by the combined action of friction (hence the advisability of a rubber lining) and centrifugal force. If a cylindrical barrel is not turning fast enough, the stones will simply stay where they are, with the stone mass sliding against the wall of the barrel. In this case the stones will be ground flat, instead of turning over and over as they should.

If the speed is too fast, stones will be carried up the wall of the tumbler rapidly and be sprayed out at the top of the tumbling mass, falling individually to the bottom of the pile with consequent fracturing or spalling. This is probably happening when you hear a knocking sound in the tumbler instead of the rumble and swish of stones tumbling end over end.

At optimum speed, the stones cascade. That is, the outer layer reaches the top of the mass and pours down the inside slope, each stone rotating as it moves.

Figure 9-1 shows what is *probably* happening in a tumbler rotating at optimum rpm. We say "probably" because no engineering studies have yet determined the effects of all the variables in the tumbling process. Consider the mass to be striated, divided into layers. Most of the grinding action actually takes place in layer B and at the layer A–B interface, as shown in Figure 9-1. The tumbling recommendations given in this book are designed to promote the formation of this layer, maintain it as long as possible and maximize its size.

If the tumbler being used is not homemade, it will probably have a constant speed. This means that additives—buffering agents and compounds to increase viscosity—will have to be used to maintain the cascading effect as the charge goes from the rough grind to the polish stage. The same effect can be achieved by varying the speed of rotation. Slowing

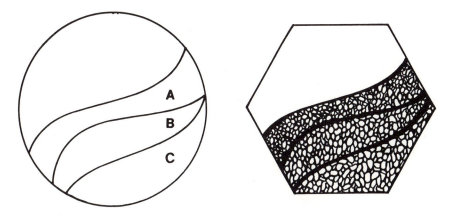

Fig. 9-1 A theoretical model of what takes place in a tumbler. *A* is a thin layer in which the stones roll or tumble over intermediate sublayer *B*. Layer *A* represents 15% of the total mass. Most grinding takes place at the *A–B* interface and throughout layer *B*, which consists of 20% to 30% of the total mass. Layer *C* is a dead layer. Although a small amount of grinding takes place near the wall of the tumbler, *C* is primarily a base layer for activity above. Sketch at right shows striated rock layers in a hexagonal barrel.

down the speed of rotation by approximately 25% in the prepolish and polish stages will achieve the same effect as thickening the slurry with sugar, as is recommended in the tables. The action is slowed, and there is less chance of chipping, breaking, spalling, edge pitting and so on.

The easiest way to slow down the tumbler for the polish stage is to use a two-speed motor with a double-pole–double-throw motor control switch between the high and low-speed windings. The low speed is about 1150 rpm and the high speed 1750 rpm on most standard electric motors.

WEIGHT AND SOLUTION VISCOSITY

Lacking speed control, solution viscosity is the major determinant of what takes place in the tumbler barrel. The amounts of additives required to give the proper viscosity are included in tumbling Tables 4–7. The quantities are for 10 pounds (4.5 kg) of stone, the actual amount of material contained in a 12-pound (5.4 kg) rated tumbler. If you have a 3-pound (1.4 kg) barrel half full, you will have about 3 pounds of stones and can cut the amounts given by about one-third. It is not necessary to weigh everything in the barrel. The weight will change slightly, according to the density of the material, or whether the pieces are large or smaller. Large pieces make a lighter load, since there is more empty space between them: thus, the differences in the amounts of abrasives necessary for large mix versus a balanced mix. Since the weight of stones is less in an even large stone mix, the weight of abrasives required will also be less. The large mix also has less overall surface area to be ground.

By including the recommended amounts of stones, abrasives and additives the slurry viscosity will be at the proper level for all the grinding stages; tumbling action shown in Figure 9-1 will be maintained for the duration of that stage. With too great a viscosity little abrasive action will take place, as if the tumbler were too full of material. If the viscosity is too low, the stones will collide violently.

The only way to actually be sure of "what's going on in there" is to control the stone mix and the amounts of additives exactly before sealing the tumbler.

The sound of the tumbler, however, will provide a rough check of the action. As mentioned, the noise of a properly loaded tumbler should be a combined swish and rumble, better remembered than described. Knocking or pinging means that the action is too violent and that stones are being chipped or spalled. Extremely quiet operation—the swish without the rumble—probably means that not enough action is taking place: stones are not rolling over and over but sliding against each other and the liner—most likely developing flat spots, if anything at all is happening. Absence of sound could also indicate that the slurry has become too thick. This may happen even in correctly charged tumblers, if the process of abrasion adds too much rock dust to the mix. Open the tumbler to make sure that the slurry is still free-flowing. In the rough grind it should feel between the fingers like heavy cream with granulated sugar in it.

CHEMICAL ACTION

Some chemical action may also be taking place in the tumbler. Most tumbling solutions are slightly acidic. Most stones contain small amounts of various metals. The result is a chemical reaction that produces a metallic salt and hydrogen gas.

We have never heard of anyone being injured by tumbler-produced hydrogen, but gas buildup can be an annoying problem. The gas pressure can become high enough to bloat a barrel with flexible walls, such as the all-rubber barrels of some smaller units, and prevent them from turning true on the shafts. In steel barrels, the gas can find its way through the seal, bringing with it some of the slurry, which not only causes a mess but also results in premature thickening of the solution.

The whole problem is easily alleviated by adding baking soda to the batch, which neutralizes the acid and helps to prevent this reaction. In

Fig. 9-2 Slurry in the rough grind should look like heavy cream.

addition to the use of baking soda, it is advisable to open the tumbler at 1 to 2-day intervals for material of this sort. Before resealing the tumbler, add more baking soda, since that which was previously added will have been neutralized.

To be on the safe side, it is probably advisable to open the tumbler away from flames and lighted cigarettes. People have been injured or killed by the explosion of hydrogen generated by storage batteries, and it is conceivable, though not likely, that a badly maintained tumbler could produce enough hydrogen to be dangerous.

BACTERIAL ACTION

Bacterial action in the tumbler can also produce gases: methane, hydrogen sulfide and other evil-smelling vapors. This usually happens when an organic material, such as sawdust or rice hulls, is used as a buffering agent. There is not much that can be done about this except to change additives or operate the tumbler in a cool place to reduce bacterial growth.

On the other hand, some natural materials, when used as additives, produce superior results. Cedar chips, the kind used for animal bedding, impart a higher luster to some materials, probably because they release minute amounts of oil. Ordinarily, any kind of oil in the batch prevents wetting of the stones and results in a poor polish; cedar oil, for some unknown reason, has just the opposite effect.

Chapter 10

Tumbling Slabs and Preforms

If most of your output of polished stones is to be used for jewelry, slabs and preforms are the most convenient shapes to set or mount. The techniques described in this chapter can also be used for the mass production of cabochons, although tumble-polished stones of this type do not have the sharply defined edges of cabochons made entirely by hand.

PREPARATION OF PREFORMS

A *preform* is any hand or machine-cut shape designed to be tumble polished. Instead of leaving the shape to chance, as when tumble polishing baroques, it is roughed out first on a diamond saw and grinding wheel, then polished to leave as much as possible of the original shape intact (Fig. 10-1).

All heels, nicks and grooves are ground smooth before the piece is put in the tumbler. If the pieces have saw marks, and most will since they are cut from sawn slabs, they must be tumbled through a rough grind of 2 to 3 days.

One way to do this is to begin with a balanced load of rough composed of the same material from which the preforms have been cut. After two or three coarse grinds, when the rough is ready to go into the intermediate stage and the slurry from the last coarse grind is almost worn down, pour in another half cup of coarse 60/90 abrasive and add the preforms to make up a maximum of 20% of the load. (An exception is very small preforms, an entire batch of which can be tumbled without other stones.)

Fig. 10-1 These crosses are fine examples of tumble-polished preforms. They were simply roughed out on a grinding wheel, then tumble polished.

Inspect the preforms every day. The objective is to remove the saw marks with the least possible removal of material from the rest of the shape.

A small preform would be a typical cabochon used in jewelry, 12 x 18 mm up to a ½-inch square, or a small slab up to 1 inch (25.4 mm) at its maximum dimension.

Tumble preforms *only* with materials of exactly the same type—obsidian with obsidian, amazonite with amazonite. (Slabs are an exception; see next section.)

Take the batch with the preforms through the rest of the tumbling process, following the instructions in Tables 4–7 for stone group F.

TUMBLING SMALL SLABS

Small slabs will generally be those cut using the cement block technique (see Ch. 14), slices of agatized coral which are often ring-shaped with a hollow center, or saw ends. They range from 2½ inches (63.5 mm) in diameter to small cabochon size (Fig. 10-2).

These slabs can be tumbled in similar material of equal hardness or in a batch of softer material, if you are concerned only with the polish on the slabs. Any slab over 1 inch (25.4 mm) in diameter is usually difficult to polish, as is any large, flat surface where contact pressure of neighboring stones is low.

Tumbling Slabs and Preforms

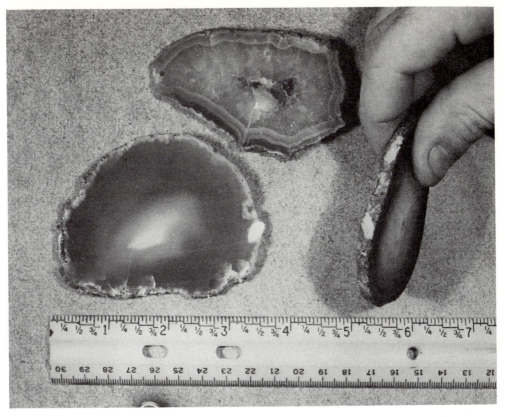

Fig. 10-2 Tumble-ready slabs.

Don't add more than 20%, by volume, of slabs to a batch. A technique to get the correct volume is to add 1½ inches (38.1 mm) of rough to the tumbler, then a single layer of slabs touching end to end to cover the rough. Place another layer of stones, a second layer of slabs and so on, until the tumbler is five-eighths full.

To ensure a good finish, there *must be no broken stones anywhere* in the batch. You could get a polish on ordinary rough if one stone in the batch were broken; this is impossible with slabs, since any broken piece will always scratch the large flat surfaces.

If the primary reason for tumbling a batch is to polish slabs only, it may be better to tumble them in a material somewhat softer than that of the slab. In the case of Brazilian agate slabs, for example, even the most minor scratches are highly visible in the polished slab. We have obtained good results by tumbling a batch of Apache Tears through two coarse grinds and then putting in the agate slabs to be tumbled, using the Apache Tears only as a carrier. One and a half or two weeks of additional rough grinding removes saw marks from the agates and also smoothes the edges, removing some of the softer matrix usually adhering to them, which might ruin the batch later on.

Apache Tears are quite a bit softer than agates. But the batch is tumbled using the materials and additives *recommended for Apache Tears*, not agates. The net result is beautifully polished slabs and hazy Apache Tears. But Apache Tears are very inexpensive, so it doesn't really matter that this material is unpolished (it can be repolished later), as long as the slabs turn out well. Or the Tears can be saved to do more slabs. The medium is ideal for tumbling hard slabs; it is softer, homogeneous in nature, relatively cheap, rounded in shape, resistant to splitting in the tumbler and will not scratch agates.

The only place scratches can originate is from other slabs in the tumbler. If the process is complete and you find scratches on a finished slab, there can be only two reasons: a broken or crumbling slab or too many slabs in the batch. You have eliminated all the variables in slab tumbling.

Fig. 10-3 Tumble-polished slabs.

The results will be astonishingly good (Fig. 10-3). The technique sounds simple, but it required a whole summer of agonizing experimentation to develop. Most other rockhounds at mineral shows had poorly polished tumbled slabs, but one or two invariably had beautiful results and they were always the ones who refused to divulge their methods. We finally found out how they did it.

Tumbling Slabs and Preforms

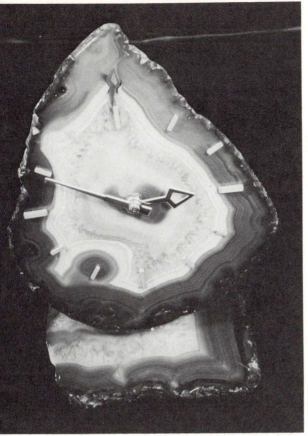
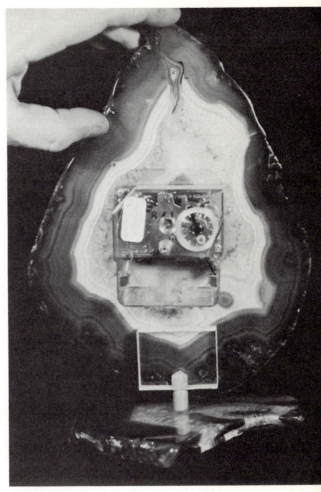

Fig. 10-4a

Fig. 10-4 (a) A tumble-polished clock face. (b) Attachment of the battery-operated clock motor.

Fig. 10-4b

TUMBLING LARGE SLABS

Slabs 3 inches (76.2 mm) and up in diameter can be tumble polished. We know of one outfit that tumble polishes slabs for clock faces: these are 6 to 14 inches in diameter, ¼ to ⅜ inch thick (152.4 to 355.6 mm diameter, 6.3 to 9.5 mm thick); see Figure 10-4 and color section. They also tumble polish slabs for other purposes, up to 1 inch (25.4 mm) thick, using 100-pound and 150-pound (45 and 67 kg) tumblers.

The lapidary puts 3 to 4 inches of tumbling medium in the bottom of the barrel to begin with, then sets the rough slabs end to end to make a complete one-slab-thick layer, as recommended for smaller slabs. By the time the tumbler is half full, the layering has produced the proper mix of slabs to medium. The larger the slabs, the thicker the intermediate layer (about one half the diameter of the large slabs). If he were tumbling 8-inch

(203.2 mm) slabs he would use 4 inches (101.6 mm) of material between layers. The medium, a balanced load of tumbled agate, is used again and again.

As mentioned earlier, the largest diameter of the slabs should be no more than 30% to 40% of the diameter of the tumbler barrel; 25% is preferable. Larger slabs *can* be tumbled, but only one at a time. (Another advantage of vibratory tumbling: we have tumbled 1-inch (25.4 mm) thick slabs that approached in size the shortest dimension of the barrel, with good results.) Follow the guidelines in Tables 4–7 for group F procedure, using Apache Tears as the medium, and plenty of plastic pellets. The pellets carry the abrasive and also help to polish the irregular surfaces on the edges of the slabs.

One thing to watch for when tumbling slabs is a piece that has been cut from a geode, then cut or broken across. A geode usually has more crystalline inclusions in the center. These will polish if the slice remains whole, but when the center material is exposed at the edge by cutting or breakage, pieces of it will continually break off during the tumbling steps. These pieces, and the rough edge of the slab itself, will have the same effect on the final polish as slivers in a standard batch. Make sure that each slice of agate has rind all around its circumference.

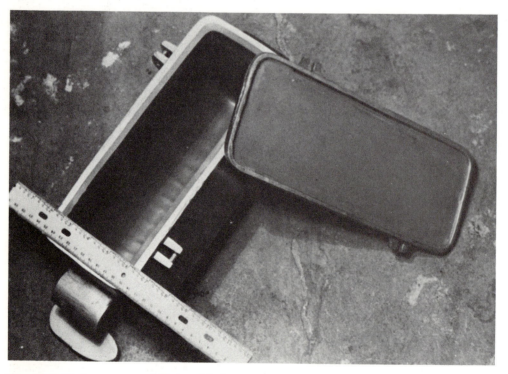

Fig. 10-5 We have successfully tumbled a 4½-inch (114.3 mm) diameter slab in the barrel of the Vibrasonic tumbler shown here. In a rotary tumbler, stones must be a *maximum* of 30% to 40% of the inside diameter of the barrel.

Tumbling Slabs and Preforms

Fig. 10-6 Commercially available slab racks are ideal for displaying finished slabs.

PREPARING SAW ENDS

Those who cut cabochons, or slab material for any other purpose, eventually wind up with a bucket full of "saw ends," the heels of stones after as many slices as possible have been cut from them. These make attractive tumbled stones. Follow the procedure recommended for small slabs and preforms, but first make sure that notches and heels from sawing are removed; if the piece contains any saw cuts, complete them before tumbling (Fig. 10-7). A notch will not polish. Break or cut off any unusable

Fig. 10-7 All notches and saw cuts should be completed before saw ends are tumbled.

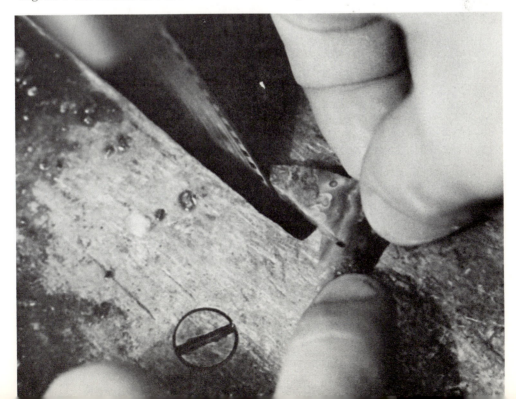

Fig. 10-8 The saw ends at left are ready to be tumbled. The saw end at right contains approximately 50% unusable material which must be removed before the piece can be tumbled. Portion to be removed has been pencil marked with an X.

portions, especially those that have pits or holes in them (Fig. 10-8). If the material was unusable for making slabs or cabochons, it will not tumble polish either.

Saw ends must be sorted for hardness and stone group before tumbling. The scrap bucket, however, will usually contain enough smaller pieces so that its contents can be tumbled as a balanced load without adding material from other sources. *Follow standard procedure.* The scrap bucket contains a percentage of good material; there is no sense in wasting these stones by ignoring good procedure, just because some of it is junk.

Tumbling Slabs and Preforms 103

Fig. 10-9 Tumbled preformed shapes.

Chapter 11

What Went Wrong?

There are bound to be some mistakes or bad batches of stones when you first begin rock tumbling. The major causes are hastiness leading to shortcuts, experimenting with new materials and lack of cleanliness. Listed in this chapter are some of the most common defects in tumbled stones, the probable causes and how to correct them.

COMMON DEFECTS AND CORRECTIVE MEASURES

Broken Stones

Breakage can occur in all stages of grinding and polishing.
Causes: Stones mishandled in washing; internal fractures completing themselves in later grind; too violent action in the tumbler from high speed or low solution viscosity.
Remedy: More care in handling; closer inspection; breaking all severe internal fractures; use of additives to increase viscosity.

No Polish

General haziness over the entire surface indicates that stones did not polish.
Causes: Confusion of polish with prepolish abrasive; insufficient additives; slurry too thin; load not large enough; mixing different stone types (soft and hard materials); carry-over of abrasive from a previous step;

What Went Wrong?

Fig. 11-1 *(Above)* Abrasives may be carried over from one stage to the next through lack of cleanliness or in more obscure ways, such as *(below)* scoring in the rubber lid of the liner or in the lip formed by the liner around the top.

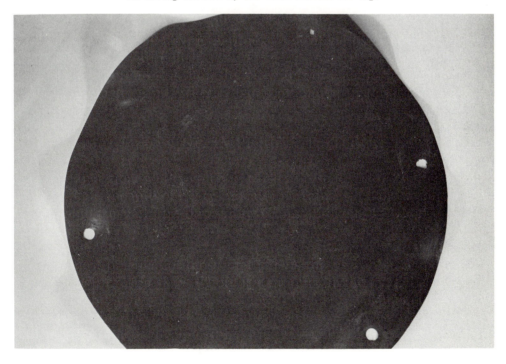

stones in the batch that have pitting or fractures which carry abrasive; stones not left in polish step long enough; bad polish.

Remedy: Keep load between one-half and five-eighths of barrel capacity; use recommended amounts of additives and thickeners; sort after each stage and remove pitted stones, splinters and broken pieces; label containers for all abrasives; use only recommended generic polishes. Test polishability of stones before stopping the prepolish step; if necessary run them through again and polish using a different compound in the polish stage. Some "polishes" on the market *will not work*. Stock tin, titanium, or cerium oxides, or (for some stones) finely divided hematite or jewelers' rouge, (see Ch. 8).

Flats

Causes: Cleavage planes of stones (no remedy); stones not tumbling, but sliding against the barrel wall.

Remedy: Increase tumbler speed; increase number of chunks in load.

Only Edges Polished

Causes: Load too far below half.

Remedy: Prepolish again, using more material or additives to bring load up to proper level. (It may be necessary to go as far back as the intermediate grind for 3 to 4 days.)

Only Centers Polished

Causes: Slurry too thin; not enough additives to carry abrasive.

Remedy: Where edge chipping is apparent, the batch must be returned to a coarse grind for 2 days, then retumbled through the subsequent stages using more thickener and additives. For minor edge chipping or more haziness at the edges, return to the intermediate grind may be sufficient.

Spalling

Figure 6-6 is a good example of spalling—pieces knocked out of the center of the stone, generally half-moon-shaped gouges.

Causes: Stones treated too harshly; not enough additives; too rapid rotation; occurs especially in a load of all large stones and in vibratory tumbling.

Remedy: Return to rough grind until all gouges are removed. Complete subsequent steps with more additives. Slow speed of tumbler rotation, if possible; if not, increase viscosity of solution slightly. Adjust vibratory tumbler to less severe action.

Incomplete Polish

When stone is shiny but lackluster, with mediocre finish, it is not completely polished.

Causes: Insufficient time in prepolish or intermediate grind; scored

What Went Wrong? 107

Fig. 11-2 Pitting, which appears in these carnelians after rough grind, can result in incomplete polish by carrying over abrasive from one step to the next. These stones would be usable if they were further rough ground to remove the surface pits. Stones with pitting should not be allowed to continue with the batch through the polish step.

barrel liner carrying abrasive from previous step; slivers left in batch (these may have been sorted out all along, but not severely enough—slivers continue to get thinner and break, abrading other stones). Incomplete barrel cleaning between stages; contamination from hidden areas between barrel liner and lid; grit on hands.

Remedy: Return to prepolish or intermediate grind.

Blistering

Surface fractures or blisters usually occur on crystalline material such as amethyst (Fig. 11-3).

Causes: Too much impact between stones because of low solution viscosity; insufficient additives; too high speed; improper handling of stones between grinds. May also be stones not sorted out of first or subsequent stages because stones were inspected when wet.

Remedy: Return to rough grind. Sort and handle carefully after surface fractures have been ground out.

Fig. 11-3 Natural internal fracturing should not be confused with the surface blistering that appears in the amethyst stones shown here.

Red Veins

Causes: Use of improper polish on materials such as feldspar that have distinct planes. Red polish collects in microscopic fractures, spoiling stone appearance (see color section).

Remedy: Try burnishing the stones once or twice with soap, as described in Chapter 8. If this doesn't work, return to intermediate grind. Follow standard procedure and finish with a white polish.

Scratch Marks

Scratches often show up on finished surfaces of flats or preforms and slabs.

Causes: Tumbling with too many other preforms and slabs in the batch; tumbling with material of same or greater hardness (single broken stone will score flats); slabs too large.

Remedy: Use maximum of 20% slabs or preforms in batch. Tumble with softer stone medium, (see Ch. 10). Tumble only slabs with a maximum dimension of 30% of barrel diameter.

Badly Finished Apache Tears

Causes: Low solution viscosity; use of filler from previous grind; leaving *any* slivers in batch.

Remedy: Return to prepolish. Remove *every* splinter or broken piece, every pellet of filler. Wash thoroughly under hard water spray. Increase amount of thickener. *Place* material carefully in tumbler. Mix water and thickener in a jar to syrup consistency before adding to batch.

No Polish Inside Irregularities or Indentations

Causes: Not enough small stones in the batch.

Remedy: Add more small stones. If tumbling an even load of all large stones, make sure sizes and shapes vary somewhat. To avoid going back to rough grind, add smaller pieces of already polished material to the batch in the prepolish stage.

Only Certain Stones Well Polished

Causes: Stones of varying hardness in a single batch. Generally only the harder stones will polish.

Remedy: Retumble softer stones with equivalent material, starting with intermediate grind (when a batch of similar material is being tumbled).

TREATING IMPERFECT STONES

Once in a great while, you may wish to rescue a stone with a fracture or one which, in spite of every precaution, refuses to take a polish. Such stones should usually be thrown away or rebroken. Touched-up stones should never be sold, but there are ways of saving such material for your own enjoyment.

The most practical of these methods is the use of clear epoxy, often used to repair broken slabs. There is a product on the market called Opticon, a very free-flowing epoxy, designed especially for this purpose. Simply by following the directions, you can disguise cracks and fractures so that they are practically invisible (Fig. 11-4). The epoxy actually penetrates the tiniest fracture before it sets. Since the material is clear and similar in refraction index to the stone, the repair is hard to detect when viewed perpendicularly.

The same type of repair can be effected with the ordinary epoxy used for mounting stones. Heat the stone first in the oven at 200° F. (94° C). Then apply a normal mix of epoxy to the fracture line. The heat of the stone will liquify the epoxy, which will be drawn into the fracture as the stone cools. Complete cure under heat, returning to 200° F (94° C) oven for 15 minutes.

Mineral oil (baby oil) will also disguise fractures for a time by wetting the rough internal edges so that they appear polished, but the effect will not last. Oil will also provide a temporary high gloss to stones such as

Fig. 11-4 A fractured slab repaired with Opticon (made by Hughes Associates).

turquoise, at the cost of eventually ruining the stone, which absorbs the oil.

Water glass, a solution of sodium silicate, can also be used to fill cracks or shallow indentations, or to make such areas appear polished. The effect of all these treatments is the same as that of wetting the stones: even rough-ground stones appear polished when wet.

Poorly polished stones can be given a high gloss with a variety of shellacs, artist's fixative, or solutions of polyethylene sprayed on the surface. All of these are temporary expedients and are easily detectable. Their effects do not last. A properly polished tumbled stone, on the other hand, will retain its luster for generations. *Don't settle for anything but the best*. Repolish poorly worked material.

What Went Wrong? 111

Fig. 11-5 Don't settle for anything but the best. Apache Tears are normally considered difficult to polish. Photograph shows a perfect polish on Apache Tears at the right and the rough material at the left.

Chapter 12

Setting Baroque Stones

Practically all baroque stones today are set with adhesives. There are other ways of setting, commercial and handmade, that provide even more beautiful effects or show off the stone to better advantage, but a tremendous variety of gold and silver jewelry can be put together simply by "gluing" the stone to the finding.

ADHESIVES

With modern adhesives, a piece of cemented jewelry can be strong, good-looking and long-lasting. The molecular bond of epoxy adhesives is often stronger than the stone or its metal finding. A tiny "up eye" held by a drop of cured epoxy resin is often used to join Apache Tears in a bracelet or necklace: if the adhesive is applied correctly, the metal links in the bracelet will bend or pull open before the cap detaches from the stone.

We have found one type of adhesive to produce consistently good results in tumbled stone jewelry. This is a two-part (resin and hardener) epoxy manufactured especially for jewelry making by Hughes Associates (Fig. 12-2). Without getting into the theory of adhesives, it is still helpful to know what characteristics to look for: a jewelry cement must be formulated for a special combination of toughness, hardness, adherence and resistance to both moisture and oil. Most ordinary household epoxies are made for a range of applications and do not have the special balance of properties required to cement stones to findings. The "instant" adhesives

Setting Baroque Stones

Fig. 12-1 Apache Tear bracelet. With modern epoxies the molecular bond—even on these highly polished stones—can be stronger than the base metal or the stone itself if the adhesive is used according to manufacturer's directions. (Hughes Associates)

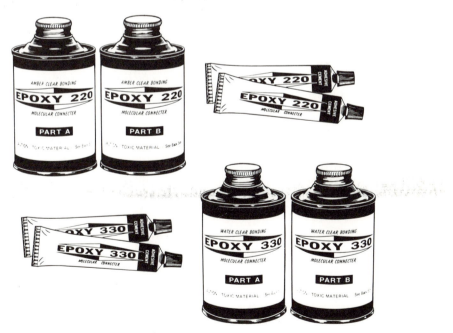

Fig. 12-2 Two-part epoxy adhesives for jewelry come in cans or tubes. (Hughes Associates)

(methyl methacrylates) used by jewelers to set pearls on prongs, while convenient, are too brittle for a mechanically unaided setting. Although they will bond two perfectly flat surfaces strongly, they will not fill gaps or voids in a less than perfect joint.

TECHNIQUES

Stone setting with a two-part epoxy is quick and easy if some elementary rules are followed.

First match your stones to their settings, choosing a side of each stone that will make contact with the metal over a wide area. The setting should be on a tray with some type of support to keep the flat surfaces level. Epoxy may thin slightly during the initial phase of the curing and, if the stone is not level on the setting, it will slide off. Settings may be supported in a tray full of sand (for heat curing), pushed into a styrofoam slab (Fig. 12-3), or held by pins or a jig on a wooden board.

Both the stones and the findings must be perfectly clean and untouched. A fingerprint can leave enough oil on the surface to prevent a strong bond. It is a good idea to wipe the surfaces with alcohol or lighter fluid just before cementing to remove all traces of grease.

Next mix exactly equal amounts of resin and hardener on a clean, nonporous surface such as an index card. If only a few stones are to be mounted, dip a toothpick into the resin and a second toothpick exactly the same distance into the hardener. Equal amounts of resin and hardener will adhere to the toothpicks. This method works best when the epoxies are bought in cans rather than tubes. The shelf life of an opened can is 8 months to a year.

The hardener and resin must be mixed thoroughly. The amount of mixing can be seen by a slight color change that occurs as the two compounds react together.

Only mix as much epoxy as you need for the stones to be set immediately. The resin does not cure completely until about 12 hours later, but after half an hour it begins to get tacky and sets in 1 to 1½ hours at room temperature.

Apply a very small amount of mixed adhesive to the level surface of the metal to which the stone is to be joined, then place the stone which you have previously sized to the finding. With small stones it is best to use a pair of tweezers for accurate placement and to avoid getting any traces of oil on the stone.

A good trick for placing small stones is to use a toothpick with a bead of beeswax on the end (Fig. 12-4). Beeswax (available at sewing or tackle shops) is just sticky enough to pick up the stone with a slight pressure. Epoxy is stickier still and when the stone is transferred to the setting holding a drop of epoxy, it will pull easily away from the wax. Placing tiny

Setting Baroque Stones

Fig. 12-3 Bracelets and capped stones mounted with epoxy are curing on a Styrofoam slab.

stones on bracelet pads is normally a tedious procedure; with the beeswax method they can be mounted as fast as the hand can move from the stone supply to the piece.

It is important not to put too much adhesive on the finding because it tends to spread out (especially if cured by heat) and is very difficult to remove after it sets. There is a solvent on the market for cured epoxy, but it is better not to make mistakes in the first place. The solvent, Attack, is usually used to remove stones from damaged findings, and is about the only relatively safe chemical that will do the job (Fig. 12-5). Epoxy is a

Fig. 12-4 A bead of beeswax on the end of a toothpick provides a convenient tool for setting small stones.

singularly impervious material, and anything that dissolves it will usually dissolve the stone, the finding and your finger as well. However, be sure to read the label and follow instructions carefully.

After the stones have been placed they should be left overnight in a level position until the epoxy has set thoroughly. Check them for slippage until the epoxy sets. The curing time can be speeded up considerably by

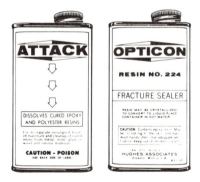

Fig. 12-5 Attack, or methylene chloride, may be used to remove cured epoxy. (Attack manufactured by Hughes Associates)

Setting Baroque Stones 117

heat. Some hobbyists use a sun lamp or merely a strong light as a mild heat source; we generally use a household oven, set at 200° F (94° C), for 15 minutes. If you use a heat source before the epoxy has set make absolutely sure that the stones are level on the finding, because epoxy becomes very liquid and slippery during the first minutes under heat, and the stones will slide off the findings at the slightest opportunity.

SELECTING AND USING JEWELRY FINDINGS

Findings—settings designed to receive stones—for baroques are available in profusion from a number of manufacturers. Some of the most popular are described and illustrated in this chapter (Fig. 12-6). Others can be made easily by hand if beauty and originality are the objectives, rather than the production of costume jewelry.

Most findings for baroques are inexpensive, made of a base metal plated with silver; silver-colored rhodium (best); imitation rhodium;

Fig 12-6 A few samples from the very large range of commercially made settings for tumbled baroques.

Hamilton gold (22 karat dip); or clad in gold, chromium or some silver electroplate or gold-colored metal. Because of their relative cheapness it pays to buy the best available grade to be sure that the plating will not chip or wear off and that it won't turn the user's finger green. The base metal may be white metal (heavy castings), steel in the cheapest settings, or brass in the best.

While we can't prescribe taste (and most certainly not what the public will buy), some care should be given to matching the stone to the findings. Silver color looks best with some stones, gold with others. Green stones—such as epidote—or black stones—onyx or obsidian—look good in oriental settings such as bamboo patterns or Chinese characters. Some stones are so attractive in themselves that the setting should be as unobtrusive as possible. Others require filigree work to bring out their patterns. Angel hair (rutilated) quartz can be highlighted by a setting with parallel lines that mimic the pattern of the crystals in the quartz. Clear stones, for example amethyst or garnet, should be set to obtain the maximum amount of transmitted light.

There are no hard and fast rules: each type of stone asks for its own setting, a fact that the American Indians realize in their handling of turquoise. A little practice and experience will soon teach even the beginner what is appropriate in terms of style, color and size. We have illustrated here some of the setting styles that have proven most popular over the years. Manufacturers are continually designing new ones; one of them may be just the thing for a new type of material. Getting on a list for catalogs of commercial findings by purchasing an order or two will keep you abreast of the many latest developments.

Listed below are some of the most popular types of findings and hints about how to use them.

Caps

The all-purpose finding for baroque gemstones is the cap. Caps attached by epoxy hold stones in amulets, pendants, bracelets and necklaces. Although a wide variety of styles is available there are two major types: the "up eye" which is shaped like a miniature bell; the bell cap, which has five or seven flat leaves that extend from the top to fit over the end of the stone. Each is somewhat conical in shape with a ring at the top to receive a separate ring or bail as a connecting link in the piece.

The up eye is the most attractive and unobtrusive, but because of its small size and surface area, requires the most care to get a good adhesive bond between the stone and the cap. When correctly applied, most of the adhesive is drawn up by capillary action into the cap so that none shows on the stone.

When applying either type of cap, push the stones to be set into a piece of Styrofoam or a tray of sand with the end to be capped upward. Make sure the cap fits reasonably well before applying the epoxy. The leaves of the cap should be bent to conform to the shape of the stone.

Setting Baroque Stones

Then apply a drop of epoxy to the inside of the cap, along each leaf, and with a pair of tweezers replace the preshaped cap on the stone. The drop of epoxy should flow between the leaves and the stone. Most beginners make the mistake of using too much epoxy. A drop, applied with a toothpick, is plenty. Any more will flow outside the leaves and make a messy-looking job.

Test the caps when the epoxy is cured. You should be unable to pull them off without breaking the stone. If you can get them off you have not mixed the epoxy properly or the stone and cap were not absolutely clean.

With the cap solidly in place you are ready to add a jump ring to fasten the stone to a chain or to connect it in a necklace or bracelet. A jump ring is simply a ring of silver or gold-colored wire cut at one point, available in a wide range of sizes. On good ones it is difficult to see where the cut has been made.

With a pair of needle-nose or jeweler's pliers (the latter are better because they will not mar the wire surface) and a pair of flat-nose pliers, open the ring *sideways*, so that the diameter remains the same (Fig. 12-7). (If the ends of the jump ring are pulled apart, you will never be able to close it properly—throw it away and use a new one.) Attach the ring to the cap and to the connecting piece and close it again, sideways. If the ring is opened and closed as shown in Figure 12-7, it will remain perfectly round, the joint will be invisible and the piece will be as strong as it can be made without soldering.

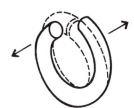

Fig. 12-7 A jump ring is opened by twisting sideways, then closed the same way.

With more advanced equipment, stones can be capped by drilling a shallow hole in the end of the stone and inserting a piece of wire which is then fixed in the hole with epoxy. Rings with short shafts for this type of mounting are available commercially or a ring can be bent from the length of wire that protrudes from the hole. The same effect is achieved by notching the end of the stone with a diamond saw and cementing the wire in the notch.

Rings

There are three general types of commercial ring settings for baroque stones: the flat pad, the cup and the wired pad, each of which has many variations.

Fig. 12-8 A pendant and earring set made by matching baroque stones in size and shape, then applying bell caps and jump rings.

With the flat pad, the stone is simply cemented to the pad—square, circular, oval or rectangular—which it should hide entirely.

The cup, with edges that protect the stone, is a more secure setting, but shows less of the material. It is best for opaque stones, unless the undersurface is so highly polished that it reflects light back through the material. It also provides a use for stones too small to mount individually. A ring cup filled with a mound of tiny polished stones, held together with clear epoxy, makes a highly attractive piece of jewelry.

Settings are often made with rings or prongs of wire attached to the pad on which the stone rests (Fig. 12-9a; also see color section). The wires are bent around the stone and seem to hold it in place. They don't. The stone is cemented to the pad and the wires are bent around it after the epoxy has set. If you try to mount the stone with the wires alone it will

Setting Baroque Stones

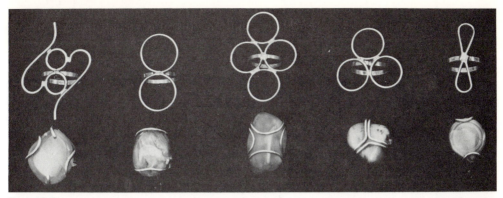

Fig. 12-9a

Fig. 12-9b

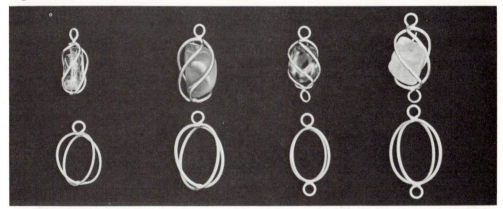

Fig. 12-9c

Fig. 12-9 Commercial sterling silver settings show great imagination in wire wrapping. (M-Line Manufacturing Co.) (a) Ring designs using wrapped stones. (b) Cuff link and earring designs. (c) Pendant designs.

remain loose in the setting; extra pressure to force the wires against the stone will only break them off the pad. This type of setting is an imitation of a method for baroque settings using stronger and more malleable silver wire. It provides the illusion that the stone is wired in place, plus providing some added protection against impact. In the sterling settings the wire actually holds the stone.

Other rings can be made by completely wrapping the stone and then soldering the wire wrapping to the ring shank. This design assures adequate strength.

Bracelets

As mentioned above, bracelets can be made from a series of capped baroques connected by jump rings and fastened with a ready-made clasp, all available from commercial findings manufacturers. Complete bracelet findings can also be purchased, with a series of cups or flat pads onto which the stone can be cemented. The mounting methods are similar to those used for rings. Sometimes the pad is larger than the stone and the texture finished to provide a sort of frame to set off the mineral color or pattern (Fig. 12-10).

One type of perennially popular bracelet has very small diamond-shaped pads for the smallest of tumbled stones. With a series of brightly colored baroques, or with stones of a single brilliant color, this bracelet is both delicate and striking.

Fig. 12-10 A three-piece set of epoxy-mounted tumbled garnets.

Setting Baroque Stones

The difficulty in making tumbled stone bracelets is to keep the pads level while the epoxy sets. The links under the pads prevent them from lying flat. Small numbers of bracelets can be made by pinning them to Styrofoam. For any greater production some sort of jig is advisable. This may be a board with grooves to accept the links. A stone sorter as shown in Figure 12-11 will be a great help in producing a batch of similar-sized stones for bracelet making.

Fig. 12-11a

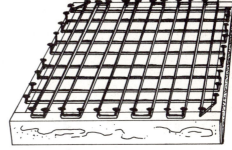

Fig. 12-11 (a) Two stone-sorting screens. The screen at the top has a mesh size of about ¼ inch (6.35mm), the other screen about ½ inch (12.7mm). (b) Sketch *(right)* shows construction of a stone sorter. The mesh is made of nylon monofilament fishing line wrapped around pins or nails in a wood or Styrofoam frame. Each crossing point of the monofilament line is secured with a drop of epoxy. Metal screens cannot be used because they mark stones.

Fig. 12-11b

Fig. 12-12 Necklace of individually wrapped baroques.

Fig. 12-13 A neck ring and pendants made with stone-clustering techniques.

Setting Baroque Stones

Necklaces

Necklaces may be made like bracelets, although the labor of affixing stones to a large number of pads makes this type of setting less common. Most baroque necklaces are made from a series of capped stones. Lately, baroque necklaces from India (beggar beads) have become quite popular. In these, the stones are drilled and strung like beads; in others, each stone is individually wrapped as in Figure 12-12.

Most large tumbled stones are used as pendants, capped or wound with wire and suspended by a chain or thong. A single capped stone can

Fig. 12-14 A filigree cross with epoxy-set stone clusters.

also be suspended from a gold or silver neckring or "dog collar" for a note of color. Others may use similar techniques with clustered stone groups instead of individually set stones.

Most manufacturers also make special pendant settings, for example a fish in which the eye is an "eye agate" fixed by epoxy. In many cases the pendant setting is designed to match a pair of earrings, using the same design, but on a larger scale (Fig. 12-15).

Fig. 12-15 Eye agate fish pendant.

Setting Baroque Stones

Earrings

Earrings, in addition to pad-type settings for small tumbled stones, offer another variation—the cage. This is usually a small sphere or similar shape made of wire to resemble a birdcage. Two of the wires are bent apart so a stone can be inserted, then bent back to their original curves. The stone remains loose but trapped inside the cage.

Attractive tumbled stone earrings can be made simply by capping a pair of similar stones—usually long, narrow ones—and fixing them to an earring finding with jump rings. Findings for pierced ears must have sterling silver (usually rhodium plated), gold or gold-filled wires. Since the wires are thin, however, precious metal earring findings are not much more costly than the plated findings used for other types of jewelry.

Pins

Manufacturers offer a wider variety of findings for pins than for any other type of tumbled stone jewelry. There is something about a pin that seems to bring out the creative, or at least the whimsical, in every jewelry designer. There are animals, reptiles, trees, fish, flowers and abstract designs, plus symbols enough to suit every holiday in the calendar and all the signs of the zodiac. On all of them, the appropriate stone is simply cemented in place.

In another type, the pin is all metal, but designed so that a capped baroque can be suspended from it.

To show the beauty of a stone, however, the best pins are made from a single, relatively flat baroque by attaching a commercial pin backing with epoxy. These pin backings, with safety catches, are made specifically for cementing to stones, and come in a variety of sizes.

Other Findings

We have illustrated other commercial findings for tumbled stones. Many more can be found in findings catalogs, including cigarette lighters, bola slides, pill boxes, cuff links, tie tacks and other jewelry items. All are made with the bonding techniques described earlier in this chapter, using either a single stone or a group of smaller stones.

Another item that has become popular in recent years is the so-called "gem tree" in which twisted wire branches are decorated with leaves and flowers of tumbled stones (Fig. 12-16). Most of these are sold in kit form, with packets of tumbled stones in the appropriate colors. Your own gemstones can be used to vary and improve the effect. Some of the trees are available as castings of easily formed alloy, and require little time to complete with stones.

Some of the larger and more beautiful gemstones may not require settings at all. They may be used for a tabletop display, a paperweight or an object on the knickknack shelf. Larger tripods of the type shown in Figure 12-17 can be used to display tumble-polished stones, small geodes or other small specimens effectively.

Fig. 12-16 Gem trees.

Setting Baroque Stones 129

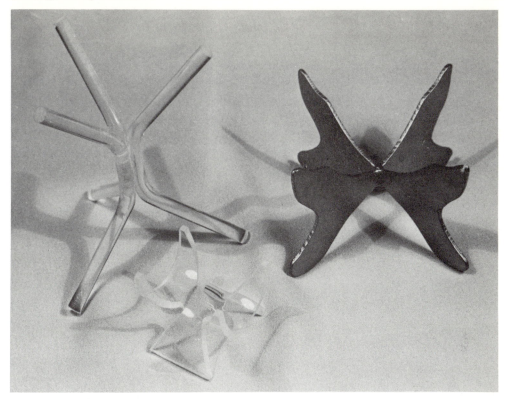

Fig. 12-17 Display stands.

LUCITE EMBEDDING

Some of the most effective tumbled stone jewelry is not made of metal at all. The stones are embedded in crystal-clear Lucite. The gemstone can be seen from every angle in full light. It retains its high polish permanently, and even a less than perfect polish is made to seem so, as the effect of embedding in plastic is the same as that of wetting the stone. The stones look as if they were suspended in air, with nothing to lessen their attractiveness (Fig. 12-18).

Some of this jewelry, when made commercially, is very costly, depending upon the skill of the designer in choosing the clear resin shapes, stone, colors and patterns, but the technique is open to anyone able to purchase an inexpensive Lucite embedding kit. Circles and rectangles can be used as pendants, simply by drilling a hole to accept a ring or pendant bail. Smaller circles make earrings, or can be set in bezels or prongs for rings. This is one way to make irregular baroques fit standard-size ring settings, if you feel so inclined. Lapidaries use this technique to make cabochons of waste materials such as opal chips.

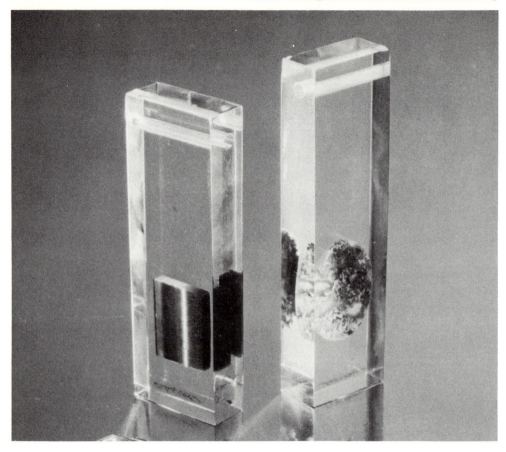

Fig. 12-18 Lucite embedding of polished semiprecious stones. Pendant at left contains tiger eye, the one at right a moss agate. (Courtesy of Sid Meyers, Clearly Stoned, Inc.)

What distinguishes the finest Lucite settings is their clarity, perfect geometrical shape (parallel faces, square edges and so on) and polish. The regularity of the setting provides an ideal contrast and frame for the irregular baroque.

Chapter 13

Handmade Baroque Settings

The methods of setting baroque stones described in this chapter are intended primarily to illustrate various ways to hold irregular stones mechanically, without prescribing any particular design philosophy. Baroque stones are used in every type of jewelry—medieval, art nouveau, geometric, primitive and so on. Once the reader has mastered various ways of caging and clamping irregular stones, he can set them in any type of design he chooses or invent new holds using the same physical principles.

Some of the settings require silver soldering. We refer the reader to *The Design and Creation of Jewelry* by Robert Von Neumann (Chilton Book Company) for a description of this technique, which can be done with a minimum of equipment. We have, however, included many designs that can be made from round 16 or 18-gauge sterling silver wire, using only a pair of pliers.

You can use your tumbler to polish silver jewelry, as well as the stones from which it was made (see Other Uses for Your Tumbler, Ch. 14).

WIRE WRAPPING

For this technique you will need 16 or 18-gauge sterling silver wire, available at jewelry supply houses and at many rock shops. It should be annealed (soft); otherwise it will be too springy to conform easily to the shape of the stone. Silver work hardens—that is, it becomes harder and more springy—the more it is bent, shaped or polished. If it becomes difficult to work while wrapping a stone, it must be heated with a propane torch until the entire length has become cherry red, then quenched in water or allowed to cool at room temperature. This is usually done on a charcoal or asbestos block, but if you have neither of these a brick will do very well. Don't worry about the heat discoloration. Silversmiths usually avoid it by quenching the wire in a "pickling" solution such as sulfuric acid instead of water, but the silver will regain its sheen during tumble polishing, even without pickling.

Now pick out a stone. For experimenting, it's best to begin with a fairly large one. A roughly cylindrical shape with a few knobs or ridges to secure the wire is easiest to wrap. Try wrapping the wire around the stone by hand until it is held securely. The trick is to use the least possible amount of wire to secure the stone without hiding it. If the curves can be made sweeping and graceful, all the better, but don't worry about form yet; once you learn to trap the stone securely, refinements in design will follow. One trick is to start with a noose of wire that can be pulled tightly around one circumference.

The stone can be wrapped like a package, in vertical and horizontal coils, in spirals or in completely irregular shapes. Experiment with wrappings that fit the shape. Once the stone is trapped in the wire, the cage can be made to conform more closely to the shape by bending with pliers and crimping.

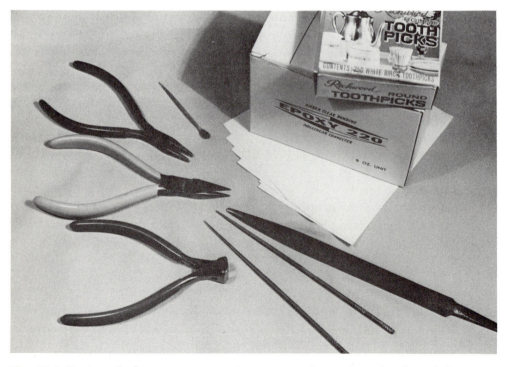

Fig. 13-1 Basic tools for stone setting. *(Left, top to bottom)* toothpick with beeswax, chain-nose pliers, jeweler's pliers and end-cutting pliers. *(Bottom right)* half-round, round and triangular Swiss-cut files.

Handmade Baroque Settings 133

Fig. 13-2 Pendant and earring set of individually wrapped stones.

Attractive settings can also be made with brass or copper wire; this is also good practice for constructing jewelry from more expensive sterling silver. Some stones may actually look better in copper or brass, but the wire should be protected against corrosion by painting it with clear nail polish or lacquer after polishing. Once your technique really becomes refined, you can use gold wire for that special piece, but it will probably have to be 18 karat or more; the 14-karat gold wire used in most jewelry feels like spring steel after working with sterling. Higher karat weights are softer but less durable. In this connection the beginner might want to try fine silver, which is more expensive but softer and easier to work with than sterling.

The typical wire-wrapped settings shown in this chapter may give you an idea of how to begin. You will soon develop your own favorite forms. The trick is to follow the contour of the stone. Learn its shape. Is it pointed at one end? Then a loop firmly crimped around that end may provide a place to begin and a purchase for further winding. Try to capture the stone with as few loops as possible.

Sterling silver wire can be purchased in a wide variety of cross sections—round, square, triangular, oval, half round, half oval, strip, channel wire and various beaded or sculptured shapes (Fig. 13-3). Round wire is the all-purpose variety for stone wrapping. Square works best for tightly crimped settings. It also has a tendency to show more prominently if the

Fig. 13-3 Cross sections of sterling silver wire available for wrapping baroque stones and for other jewelry uses.

wire wrapping is to be an integral part of the design. Twisting it produces a series of sparkling surfaces that draw the eye even more.

The half-round and half-oval forms may be used for close contact with the stone surface and also as claws in some of the soldered settings illustrated (Fig. 13-4).

Other wire shapes provide still more interesting effects. If you plan to set many stones it is a good idea to buy a few feet of each type of wire to experiment with. Channel wire, with a U-shaped cross section, is useful for holding stones that have a thin edge all the way around, such as tumble-polished slabs. The wire is bent to conform exactly to the edge of the stone, leaving a gap between the ends of about ⅛ inch (3.17 mm). The wire is then removed and ½-inch (12.7-mm) length of 16-gauge round wire soldered inside both ends of the channel wire so that about ⅜ inch (9.5 mm) shows in the gap. When the channel wire is replaced on the stone, the round wire is formed into a loop to receive a chain, drawing the channel wire tightly around the edges of the piece.

An interesting setting for very rounded stones, difficult to trap in wire, can be made from ¼-inch (6.3 mm) or wider silver strip. A Moebius Strip, the famous one-sided figure, can be made by bending it in a circle and twisting one end 180° so that the back of one end joins the front of the other (Fig. 13-5). Try it with paper first. Make it large enough so that one lobe of the figure is slightly smaller than the stone. When the round gemstone is inserted, the figure will dilate to receive it. To make the hold completely secure, add a drop of epoxy inside where it can't be seen. We suggest that this setting be made with fine silver which can be bent more easily into complex curves without buckling.

Ancient silversmiths decorated their work with twisted silver wire. They wrapped sword handles with it; you can wrap stones. The technique is easy and strangely satisfying. Use a hand drill with a hook made of coathanger wire and a small vise. Take a piece of 18-gauge or smaller wire, bend it in half and insert the two ends close together in the vise. Hook the end of the loop and turn the drill and you will have a perfect, completely uniform twist. An astounding variety of patterns can be made by this means, using different numbers of wires and different cross sections. The braid holding the agate in Figure 13-6 was made by twisting one pair of wires to the right, a second pair to the left, then twisting both together to the right.

Heavier 16-gauge twisted wires can form a cage for baroque stones.

Handmade Baroque Settings

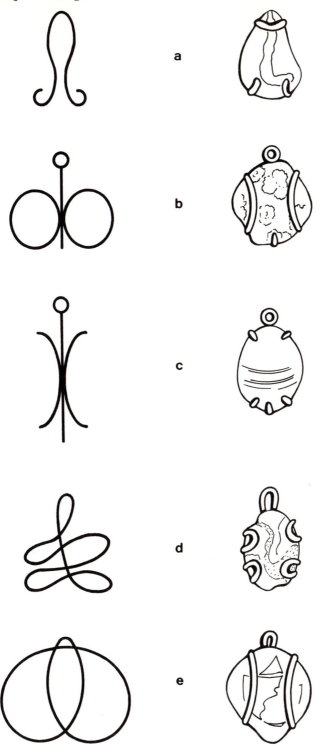

Fig. 13-4 (a—e) Silver wire forms, before *(left)* and after *(right)* stone setting.

Fig. 13-5 A piece of rose quartz held in a wrapping of silver known as a Moebius strip.

Twist four or five wires, slightly longer than the longest dimension of the stone. Then untwist slowly until the wires bow out into a cage similar to that shown in Figure 13-7. Insert the stone and close the wires around it, being careful to maintain the original sweeping curve of each. The ends may be fastened by soldering or with a wrapping of smaller gauge wire that also forms a loop for attaching the piece. You might also want to try a short length of silver tubing, just large enough for all the wires to pass through. Bending the protruding ends down around the tubing will hold the piece together securely without soldering. This type of cage, made with straight rather than twisted wire, looks vaguely like a sea anemone.

Other cages, in which a stone fits loosely, can be made from spirals of wire. Two joined together form a spherical cage. The spiral is formed by coiling round or square wire with pliers or by winding around a pin held upright in a vise. When the center winding of the coil is pulled downward, it becomes an even spiral. A long, icicle-shaped spiral of twisted square wire is an attractive finding for baroque earrings.

Handmade Baroque Settings

Fig. 13-6 Agate pendant made from braided silver wire.

Fig. 13-7 Sterling silver wire stone cages.

SHEET METAL SETTINGS

Sterling silver, copper, bronze or aluminum sheet metal is even more versatile than wire for setting baroque stones. All you need is a pair of tin snips for the simpler shapes. The more complex require a jeweler's saw for making internal cuts. Many of the settings shown here can be made without soldering.

The use of sheet metal can provide a wide variety of textures as well as shapes. The metal can be hammered, chased with a pointed tool, pierced, scored, engraved, or even reticulated (heated with a torch until the surface becomes wrinkled).

Most of the settings shown here can be made with 18-gauge sheet (Fig. 13-8). You can use heavier or lighter gauges, depending upon the size of the stone to be mounted.

Tension mounts made from sheet are good for small stones, as in earrings. In a tension mount, the springiness of the metal is used to capture the stone. Find two similarly shaped stones, preferably with pointed ends.

Cut two teardrop-shaped pieces of sheet, both wider and longer than the stones, leaving a tail of metal on the top to form a ring. Make a pocket

Handmade Baroque Settings

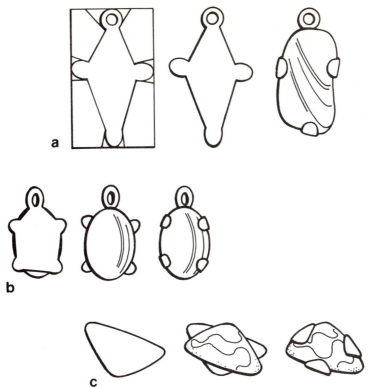

Fig. 13-8 (a, b, and c) Sheet-metal settings requiring no soldering. *(Front left)*: sheet metal, sheet metal after cutting, sheet metal folded over stone.

or a cutout in the top and the bottom of the shape into which the ends of the stone will fit, then curve the piece until, from top to bottom, it is shorter than the stone. The ends of the stone should snap into the pockets and be held there by spring tension. If the hold is not tight enough, use a drop of epoxy in each indentation.

Stones with relatively narrow edges can be held in a band of sheet metal. The band is made the same circumference as the stone and the edges are crimped down on both sides with a pair of pliers. The raised sections left after crimping can be filed away to leave a scalloped edge (Fig. 13-9) or cut down entirely so that the band follows the contour of the stone. This type of setting is particularly good for slabs that have been cut on a diamond saw and then tumble polished (see color section).

Claw settings for irregular stones are easily made from sheet, although the technique works best on those that have one fairly flat side. Lay the stone on a piece of sheet and trace the outline. Then mark where you want the claws to be and cut out the piece with tin snips, leaving tabs in three or four places to form the claws and ring (if a pendant). The tabs can be any shape you like—just make sure that they are long enough to reach over the top, otherwise you will not be able to get the stone tight in its setting (Fig. 13-10).

Fig. 13-9 A slab of Botswana agate in a crimped silver sheet metal setting.

The tabs are bent over the stone and forced down with a burnishing tool or pliers. Since the backing of the piece is a flat sheet of silver, this type of setting is particularly good for pins and, when used with smaller stones, is suitable for baroque rings.

A more elegant, but difficult, setting is shown in Figure 13-11. It is best to use a fairly small, flat stone for this. Cut a piece of sheet larger than the stone and in the center outline the baroque as you would for a sheet metal setting with tabs. Then mark the outline in six or eight segments, as

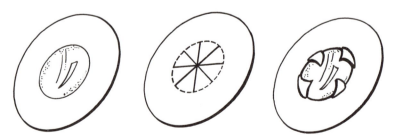

Fig. 13-10 Sketch shows method of cutting out prongs on sheet metal setting.

Handmade Baroque Settings

Fig. 13-11 A Botswana agate set into a triangle of sterling using technique in Figure 13-10.

if slicing a pie. Drill a hole in the center and, with a jeweler's saw, cut the segments up to (and a little beyond) the outline of the stone.

You will be left with an even number of triangular prongs. Alternate prongs should be bent up on either side of the sheet. The stone is then inserted and the prongs pushed down on both sides, trapping the stone within the metal.

BUILT-UP SETTINGS

Once you have mastered the art of silver soldering, the number of possible settings for baroque stones is endless. We have included a few of the most popular types here; each can be made with a pair of pliers and a propane torch. One additional requirement is a block of charcoal or asbestos.

Fig. 13-12a

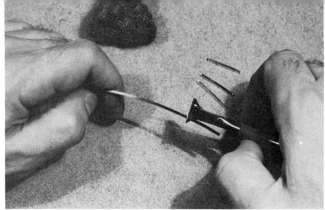

Fig. 13-12b

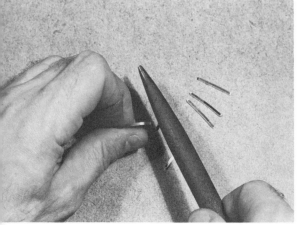

Fig. 13-12c

Fig. 13-12d

Fig. 13-12e

Fig. 13-12f

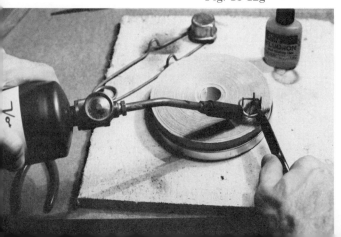

Fig. 13-12g

Fig. 13-12h

Handmade Baroque Settings 143

Fig. 13-12 (a) Steel wool being used to clean the silver. It should also be used on the solder. (b) Diagonal end nips cut the lengths of silver. (c) Rough-cut ends are filed flat so that they will fit closely in the ring section. (d) Pieces being fitted together and aligned for soldering. (e) Pieces in place on the solder block. The prongs are pressed into the block about halfway so that they extend an equal distance on either side of the ring. (f) Applying flux to the piece before soldering. (g) Soldering with a propane torch. (h) The piece after the prongs have been bent around the stone, filed to shape and polished.

Fig. 13-13 Another prong setting.

Fig. 13-14 Fish-shaped pendant of square sterling silver wire with half-round prongs holding a piece of Brazilian agate.

The fish shape shown in Figure 13-14 is made by hand bending a piece of square wire (16-gauge or heavier). The width of the body should be about ⅛-inch (3.17 mm) larger than the stone to be set. The shape is then laid on an asbestos or charcoal block, with the stone in place, and pieces of round or half-round wire pushed into the block in the space between the stone and the surrounding wire. The wire pieces that will form the prongs holding the stone should be long enough to bend securely over each side. If half-round wire is used, the flat side should face the stone. The prongs are pushed far enough into the charcoal or asbestos so that half their length shows above the surrounding wire. They should be placed at points where they can be bent securely around the edge of the stone.

Handmade Baroque Settings

The stone is then removed and the wire pieces soldered to the outline. At the same time the two ends forming the tail of the fish are soldered together and a ring to hold the pendant joined to the "nose." The tendency is to solder the ring in the same plane as the fish. This means that another jump ring must be added for the pendant to hang straight. Instead, try joining the ring perpendicular to the plane of the piece (Fig. 13-15).

Some variations of this technique are shown, using twisted wire instead of square and following the contour of the stone rather than an abstract shape. As many prongs as necessary can be added.

Fig. 13-15 A Brazilian agate in a picket bezel setting (a form of sterling silver available from jewelry supply houses). Note that the ring is soldered perpendicularly to the picket bezel so that the necklace chain can be applied directly to the piece without a jump ring.

Fig. 13-16 A ring made from a multiple-prong setting. The stone is Botswana agate.

The Botswana agate ring in Figure 13-16 is made from a heavy (10-gauge) half-round wire surrounded with a dozen prongs. The prongs were pushed very deep into an asbestos block and the long ends were bent completely around the bottom of the stone to form a support for the ring shank, which is also made from 10-gauge half-round wire. A small plate of sheet silver was soldered to the back to join all the prongs and provide a firm resting place for the ring shank.

The ring shown in Figure 13-17 is a variation of the cage setting. It consists of four rings of 16-gauge wire, two of the desired ring size and two that are about two sizes larger (as measured on a ring mandrel). All four rings are soldered together at one point on the bottom. Two-thirds of the way up the ring shank on each side are soldered two spacers that hold the four wires in a cage form suitable for a small baroque or a Herkimer diamond.

These are merely a few examples of baroque settings that can be made by anyone with a minimum of experience and the simplest of tools.

More sophisticated jewelry-making techniques available today, such

Fig. 13-17 A variation of the cage setting, made as a ring and holding a Herkimer diamond.

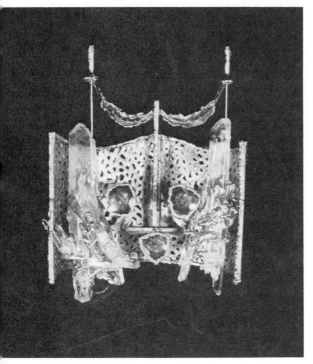

Fig. 13-18a

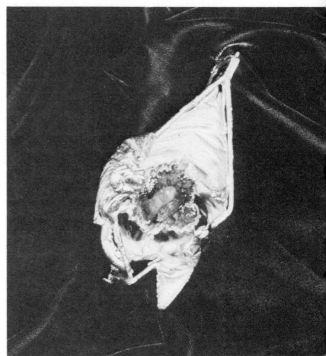

Fig. 13-18b

Fig. 13-18 Electroformed jewelry, courtesy of Helen Drutt Gallery. (Photos by Photo Associates, Philadelphia) (a) Toque: electroformed gold on silver with watermelon tourmaline slabs and quartz crystals by Stanley Lechtzin. (b) Brooch: electroformed silver gilt and quartz crystals by Stanley Lechtzin. (c) Neckpiece: electroformed silver, plastic and quartz crystals with photo-fabricated image by Eleanor Moty.

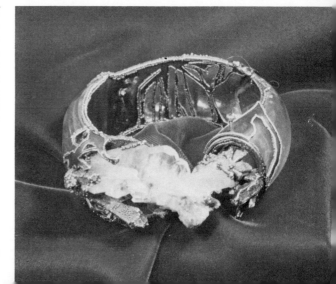

Fig. 13-18c

as lost wax casting and electro-deposition of precious metals, are eminently suited to mountings in which the stone, no matter what its shape, can actually be embedded in the metal (Fig. 13-18).

"Gloppies" or drop castings of silver also make interesting settings for baroques. The latter are simply irregular shapes of silver made by melting the metal in a hollow on the charcoal block and then dropping it rapidly into ice water. By controlling the depth of the water, its coldness and the height above the water where the metal is released (this takes some experimentation), the resulting shape can be made concave, almost a half sphere, just right for holding an odd-shaped stone.

It is hoped that this chapter has introduced methods which may be varied or improved upon by the individual hobbyist. Remember, however, that unless you are producing a single type of setting, the labor involved in the handicraft, if you place a value on your time, makes such individually wrought pieces prohibitively expensive when compared to ready-made settings. Once in a while, however, you may come across the rare stone that is so perfect it demands its own individual place. Then use as much time, imagination and craftsmanship as you possess to show it off to best advantage.

Chapter 14

Other Tumbler Uses and Auxiliary Equipment

If you decide to use some of your baroque stones to make handmade silver jewelry, the rock tumbler can save a great deal of time, effort and expensive equipment. Ordinarily, any silver jewelry that has been subjected to heat must be pickled in an acid solution to remove soldering flux or fire scale, then buffed with Tripoli and finally finish polished with jeweler's rouge.

When done by hand, these steps can be extremely time consuming, but mechanical buffing equipment may not be worth the expense if you plan to make only a few pieces. Furthermore, there is always the hard-to-get-at internal surface that is almost impossible to polish by hand *or* machine (many silversmiths black these out with a silver oxidizing solution).

BURNISHING FINISHED JEWELRY

The tumbler is the answer to all these problems. It works so well that it is almost a jeweler's trade secret. The only additional material you will need is tumbling shot, shown in Figure 14-1. This may be difficult to find in your local rock shop or jewelers' supply house. If so, it can be ordered by mail from Swest, Inc., 10803 Composite Drive, Dallas, Texas 75220.

Tumbling shot consists of a variety of highly polished stainless steel shapes—cones, balls, rods, saucers and needles. These shapes do not grind a metal surface, but rather burnish it.

Simply place the piece of silver to be polished into a 3-pound (1.4 kg) tumbler one-third to one-half full of shot, a cup of detergent and 2

Fig. 14-1 Tumbling shot—highly polished stainless steel shapes.

Other Tumbler Uses and Auxiliary Equipment

Fig. 14-2 Tumbler charged with shot, soap and silver shapes.

tablespoons of Tripoli or tin oxide. Fill the tumbler as if you were charging it with rock—that is, with shot, detergent, metal piece and polish, and water up to the top layer (Fig. 14-2).

Tumble for an hour or two, then inspect. Most pieces by this time will have a beautiful burnished finish, even in those hard-to-reach places (Fig. 14-3). If the piece is very badly stained or tarnished, it may have to be left in the tumbler longer. Or, as an alternative, some polishing compound, such as cerium oxide (don't use rouge, it is too difficult to clean off), can be added to the batch without harming the silver or the shot.

Since this is a burnishing process which polishes a surface by exerting pressure rather than removing metal, it will not remove file or saw marks. It *will* get rid of just about everything else.

We have seen silversmiths working at the bench and simply dropping each piece into an open-topped (angled) tumbler hot from the torch.

Fig. 14-3a

Fig. 14-3b

Fig. 14-3 (a and b) Difficult-to-polish silver shapes before (a) and after (b) polishing with tumbling shot and soap.

Other Tumbler Uses and Auxiliary Equipment

TUMBLING OTHER MATERIALS

Shot tumbling works just as well with other metals as with silver. In addition to polishing gold, silver, brass or copper jewelry, it will also remove rust and corrosion from small metal parts for the home handyman.

Tumbling with abrasive is a method that can be used to round and smooth almost any material. Why not experiment on your own? For example, small pieces of driftwood make excellent bases for stone displays, rock bugs, etc. Although we have not tried it, there's a good possibility that tumbling with a very coarse abrasive, or even sand, could make "instant driftwood" out of irregularly shaped pieces of lumber or even trimmed, dried branches. Once these are dried in the sun, they should be indistinguishable, except for the salt smell, from wood tumbled for years in the waves.

DIAMOND SAWS

Probably the most useful adjunct to a rock tumbler is a diamond saw. It will cut preforms—crosses, rectangles, diamonds—for tumbling; make slabs, which also tumble polish very well; groove or notch baroques for handmade settings; slice single stones into two similarly shaped halves for earrings. As you get deeper into the lapidary hobby, you will find myriad additional uses for this piece of equipment.

Diamond saws are not expensive. Small bench models (trim saws) are available from $30 to $60, considerably less than the cost of a good vibratory tumbler.

Trim Saws

This type of saw consists of a worktable slotted for a diamond blade mounted on an arbor (Fig. 14-4). The arbor is equipped with a sheave for V-belt drive from a separate motor. The setup is similar to a table-mounted circular saw. The difference is that the diamond saw is considerably safer. Your fingers can press against the edge of the rotating blade without damage.

The diamond saw is actually not a saw at all, but a very rapid-cutting grinding wheel formed of diamond particles embedded in the outer rim of a steel disk.

When the saw is running, a coolant must be applied to the blade to carry away heat and rock cuttings. In the small trim saw, the lower fraction of the blade is immersed in the coolant and carries enough of it around to the workpiece to do the job. The more expensive models have a sump and an electric pump that applies the coolant to the blade under pressure.

The coolant is usually four parts kerosine mixed with one part motor oil. Transmission fluid is a good lubricant since it is relatively odorless, but you can use any additive-free crankcase oil. Water soluble oils are also available, but the kerosine mixture is preferable, especially if the blade remains idle for more than a week at a time. Water-soluble oils will not corrode most metals, but the rim of a diamond saw is under stress and, when immersed for very long in water-soluble oils, it is subject to a type of attack known as stress corrosion cracking. The blade is the most expensive part of a diamond saw, so if water-soluble oils are used, it is a good idea to take the blade off the machine and dry it if the saw is not going to be used for some time.

Some materials, such as opal or turquoise, absorb oil and must be cut

Fig. 14-4 Various models of diamond trim saw: (a) six-inch saw (Star Industries); (b and c, Ferrara Industries).

Fig. 14-4a

Fig. 14-4b   Fig. 14-4c

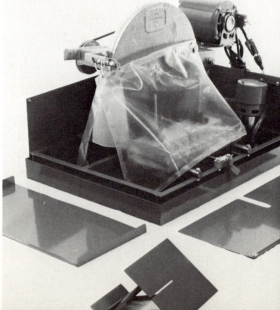

Other Tumbler Uses and Auxiliary Equipment 155

with water alone as a coolant. In this case, the entire machine must be drained, cleaned and dried after use.

Note: It is advisable to wear a respirator or dust mask when operating a diamond saw in an enclosed area, since the coolant disperses into the air as a fine mist.

The trim saw is useful and economical, but has one drawback: it has no provision for cutting uniform slabs. A vise is generally included to hold large stones during the cutting, but there is no provision for indexing it. Once a piece is cut from the stone, there is no way of indexing—moving the remainder a small distance forward to cut an even slice parallel to the first cut—except to loosen the vise, move the stone by hand and tighten the vise again. Slabs cut in this way are likely to be uneven.

Fig. 14-5 Fourteen-inch swing-arm diamond slab saw.

Fig. 14-6a

Fig. 14-6b

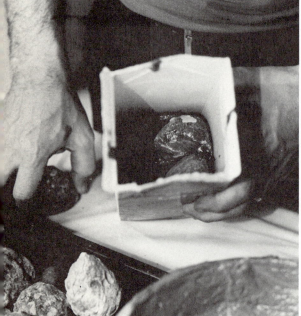
Fig. 14-6c

Fig. 14-6d

Slab Saws

The best arrangement we have seen for indexing is on the Lortone 14-inch (355.6 mm) diamond saw, a unit that sells for a very reasonable price (about $200), considering its size and versatility (Fig. 14-5). On this saw the blade moves up and down on a swing arm. The arm is threaded, with a crank on one end. One turn of the crank moves the blade sideways 1/16 inch (1.58mm). The rock is clamped in a vise below the saw blade. After the first cut the blade is moved sideways, say ¼ inch (6.35 mm), and a second cut is made, resulting in a perfectly even ¼-inch-thick slab.

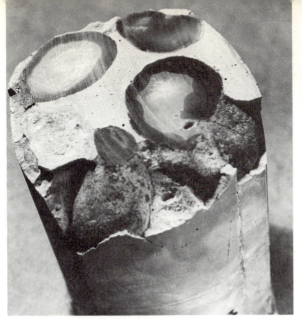
Fig. 14-6e

Fig. 14-6f

Fig. 14-6g

Fig. 14-6h

Fig. 14-6 Formation of cement block for cutting small slabs. (a) Measuring cement. (b) Cement is mixed to soupy consistency. (c) Placing stones in cardboard milk carton. (d) Unwrapping hardened cement block. (e) Use block within two months or it will begin to crack. (f) Block being sliced on slab saw. (g) Cement being broken away from agate slabs. (h) Pliers may be necessary to break cement.

SLABBING SMALL STONES

Small stones can be slabbed with an indexing saw or a trim saw by using cement. (Agatized coral is one material that is greatly improved by slabbing prior to tumbling.)

Mix a small batch of portland cement *without sand* to a fairly soupy consistency (Fig. 14-6 a and b). Then take a ½-gallon milk carton and begin to fill it with the stones to be slabbed (Fig. 14-6c). Put in one layer of stones so that the cut will be across their smallest diameters (or wherever you think the best pattern will result), then add enough cement to cover the stones and fill in the spaces between them. Add the next layer of stones, more cement, and so on, until the carton is full. Leave about 2 inches (50.8 mm) of plain cement on the top. This will permit the stones in the carton to be slabbed while still leaving a portion of the block to be gripped by the saw vise. Knead and agitate the carton until the cement fills all the spaces, and let it set for a day or two. Then peel the carton away from the cement block (Fig. 14-6d). The cement will be hard enough to hold the stones for slabbing after drying overnight. Do not save the blocks too long before cutting, since they will begin to crumble (Fig. 14-6e).

Even the smallest stones can be cut into slabs in this way, as long as the outer surfaces are rough (Fig. 14-6f). Polished stones or those contaminated with oil will not be held by the cement and may turn and damage the saw blade.

Usually the cement will break away easily from the cut slabs (Fig. 14-6g). If it does not, a little gentle pressure with a pair of pliers will do the trick (Fig. 14-6h). The rough-sawed slabs can then be tumble polished, following the recommendations in the chapter on tumbling slabs and preforms. Slabs cut in this way are generally devoid of heels and chipped edges. They are tumbler ready!

Slabs and preforms cut on a trim saw should be cleaned up before tumbling to remove "heels" left by sawing, feathers and sharp edges that may crack easily in the tumbler.

NOTCHING AND GROOVING

Other uses of the diamond saw in making baroque jewelry include notching and grooving (Fig. 14-7). As mentioned in the chapter on handmade settings, stones can be joined in a necklace or bracelet by cutting a notch in each end, slightly deeper than the wire that is to form the connecting ring, then cementing sections of wire in these notches. The projecting end of the wire is bent to form the connecting ring. (Jump rings can also be cemented in directly.)

Prong settings of baroque stones can be made much stronger and more secure by cutting notches in the stone at points where the prongs are to be placed. These notches can also be ground in using the sharp shoulder of the grinding wheel, but the diamond saw does a much neater job.

One of the easiest ways of hand-setting an irregular stone is to make a groove with a diamond saw completely around its circumference (Fig. 14-8). A wire, or series of smaller wires, is wound in the groove and twisted at the top to form a ring. Slabs should be grooved prior to tumbling, using only slabs ⅜ inch thick. (Only hard materials can be grooved in slabbed form.) Many hobbyists consider this too much work and would rather use bell caps. Professionals, who depend largely on technique to

Other Tumbler Uses and Auxiliary Equipment 159

Fig. 14-7 Notching a baroque on a trim saw.

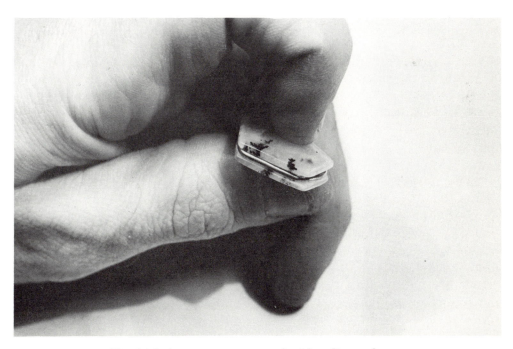

Fig. 14-8 A moss agate grooved with a diamond saw.

produce pieces which command higher prices, never consider the tumbled gem to be simply another mass polished stone to be slapped into a cheap mount.

CUTTING PREFORMS

The indexing saw described earlier has another attachment highly useful in rock tumbling, the preform attachment. This is a simple fixture of steel or aluminum that fits in the stone vise and guides a slab of material. Parallel cuts which nearly penetrate the slab are made across the entire slab surface once an initial groove has been made.

The saw blade is equipped with a stop so that it does not cut entirely through the slab nor come in contact with the metal base. With the slab guided by the lip of the fixture, a series of parallel cuts can be made in the slab either by indexing the blade or indexing the slab in a previously cut groove. Then the slab is turned and another series of cuts made at any angle to the original. The result is a large number of precise shapes—squares, rectangles, triangles or diamonds—which, when tumble polished, make very desirable gemstones for jewelry from cuff links to earrings.

The pieces are easily broken from the slab by hand, or with a pair of pliers if necessary, and the edges cleaned up slightly on the grinding wheel before tumbling.

More complex preforms will have to be cut manually. The outline is drawn on a slab with an ordinary graphite pencil, either freehand or using a template available for this purpose. It would be a good idea to begin with shapes made of straight lines. Curves should not be cut on a diamond saw. The curved piece is roughly cut from a slab by using a series of straight saw cuts. The piece is then ground on a 220-grit wheel to obtain the desired curvature. Final grinding and polishing can then be achieved by tumbling.

GRINDING WHEELS

Grinding is a process best done on another piece of auxiliary equipment, a wet grinding wheel (Fig. 14-9). Many models of grinders are available as lapidary equipment, or one can be improvised from an ordinary bench grinder. All that is necessary is some provision for keeping the grindstone wet. The old-fashioned axe grinder, with a drip can at the top of the wheel, would be ideal for occasional stone grinding. The best all-purpose wheel for cleaning up preforms, or flattening the backs of baroques before setting, is a 220-grit Carborundum wheel specifically made to be used wet.

Do not try to grind stones on a dry wheel. It will work for some stones,

Other Tumbler Uses and Auxiliary Equipment

Fig. 14-9a

Fig. 14-9b

Fig. 14-9 Typical lapidary grinder-polisher: (a, Star Diamond Industries, Inc.); (b) Grinder-polisher with trim saw.

but most will crack and pieces of the edge will break away. In addition, some stones produce a toxic dust, depending on their mineral composition. If you do not have a wet grinding wheel and have only a few pieces to do, edges can be rounded and small projections removed by hand with wet 320-grit emery cloth.

DRILLING HOLES

At some point in the tumbling craft, the hobbyist may need to drill a hole in a stone to attach it to a piece of jewelry in some way. There are several ways to do this, most of them tedious. You can use a bow drill and grit like the ancient Egyptians, but a high-speed flexible shaft or handheld drill is faster.

The cheapest method, if only a few stones need to be drilled, is to use a piece of 1/32" steel from a hypodermic needle or 1/16" silver tubing as the drill bit. The stone to be drilled is mounted in plaster or cement, and left in the container that formed the mold (Fig. 14-10). Leave enough of the container, ½ to ¾ inch (12.7–19.05 mm), to provide a reservoir for coolant water required for drilling. Alternatively, when drilling a slab, a dam can be made of modeling clay around the point to be drilled, or the entire slab can be mounted in a foil coolant container fashioned by hand.

The business end of the tubing where it touches the stone can be cut with a jeweler's saw or scored if you like to hold more abrasive. This may start the hole faster, but the score marks, unless very deep, will be worn away before you get very far into the stone.

In the dam, mix up a free-flowing slurry of coarse grit and water. The abrasive, forced against the stone by the tubing, does the actual drilling while the tubing merely carries abrasive and applies pressure. The drill should be lifted and let fall gently against the stone every few seconds with a "pecking" motion, to allow fresh grit to run under the bit. Do not apply excessive pressure.

The interchangeable stone ring shown in Figure 14-11 was made with flat tumbled stones drilled by this method. Each hole took approximately half an hour to drill, through stone less than 3/16-inch (4.7 mm) thick. The stones were hard—jasper and epidote—but even with softer materials, drilling is a time-consuming process.

Drilling Machine

A more advanced system, which uses "free flowing" abrasive slurry pumped through the drill bit, and supplied through a special collar which holds the bit, is available commercially. This system with pumps, tubing, and collar has a cost closely approximating an automatic cam-operated rock drill.

An even more advanced system, one of the most highly sophisticated

Other Tumbler Uses and Auxiliary Equipment 163

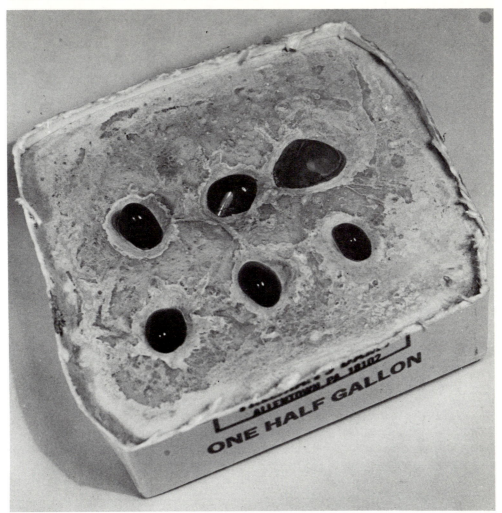

Fig. 14-10 Stones set in cement to be drilled.

of all, is the ultrasonic drilling device. It also uses loose abrasives, which are automatically fed to the drill bit. Drilling speed for 1/16-inch (1.58 mm) holes in hard agate is approximately ¼ inch (6.35 mm) per minute. The cost in this case is $1000 to $2000 per unit, which is getting into the area of latest development—the laser drill!

Drilling with inexpensive, fixed drill-bit machines can be speeded up considerably by using a diamond drill bit (Fig. 14-12). These bits are available in a wide variety of shapes and sizes (usually for stone carving) for $1.50 to about $6 per bit, depending on the size and the quality of the embedded diamond particles. These bits must be used wet like the tubing, but at much higher speeds, as recommended by the manufacturers.

Fig. 14-11 Sterling silver ring with interchangeable stone (drilled).

Cam-operated Drill

Diamond bits can be used also on cam machines, which provide a pecking motion allowing chips and ground stone to clear the hole during drilling.

The machine shown drilling a slab in Figure 14-13 provides the proper motion automatically. It will do the job unsupervised. But unless one plans to drill a large number of tumbled stones for beads or slabs for use as pendants, it is probably not a worthwhile investment for the non-professional (automatic machines cost approximately $130).

Other Tumbler Uses and Auxiliary Equipment

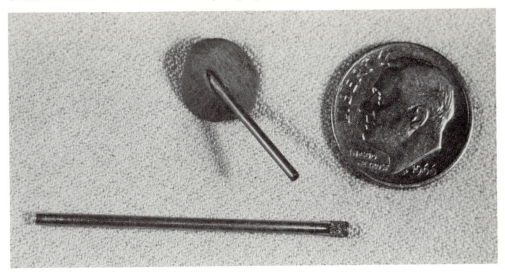

Fig. 14-12 A diamond bit (below) and a piece of steel tubing used for drilling stones.

Fig. 14-13 (a) Automatic rock drill. (b) Drilling a slab with an automatic rock drill.

Fig. 14-13a

Fig. 14-13b

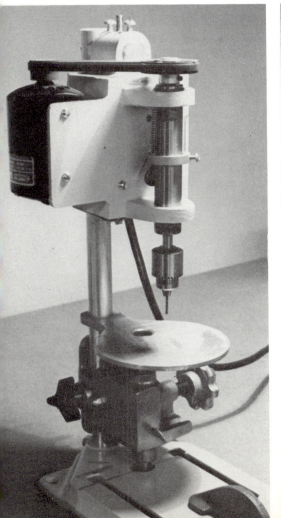

Appendix

Commonly Tumbled Stones: Characteristics and Folklore

Agate

Microcrystalline quartz in which the crystals are oriented in bands. Hardness 7. There are thousands of varieties of agate, distinguished by color, pattern, type of banding and inclusions (moss agate). "Eye agate," in which the banding pattern forms "eyes" of lighter color against a dark background, was once thought to protect the wearer against the evil eye. Various types of agate have been said to guarantee success in love or business, promote courage and prevent insomnia, while agatized coral was believed by some medieval alchemists to counteract the force of gravity.

Amethyst

A purple variety of crystalline quartz. Hardness 7. Once a precious stone, the discovery of large deposits in South America (Brazil) has reduced its value to semiprecious, although the finest grades are still faceted and set in diamonds. Its principal virtue during the middle ages was to protect the wearer against drunkenness, from either liquor or love, and, as a corollary, to induce clear thinking.

Bloodstone

A form of dark-green microcrystalline quartz with red inclusions. Hardness 7. An easy stone to tumble polish, bloodstone was once, like amethyst, more precious than it is today. The larger the flecks of "blood" the better the grade. The stone was thought to stop bleeding when pressed against a wound, and to neutralize poison. Its possessor could also produce thunderstorms, in the sighing of whose winds he could read oracles of the future.

Carnelian

Red or reddish white chalcedony. A form of microcrystalline quartz. Hardness 7. Worn by the Prophet Mohammed, the stone was said to have the power of averting envy and imparting courage. It was also supposed to protect the wearer from falling roofs or walls.

Chalcedony

A microscopically crystallized variety of quartz (silicon dioxide), in which the crystals are arranged in parallel bands of slender fibers. Hardness 7. The variety most often tumbled ranges in color from milky to sky blue. The stone is supposed to drive away ghosts or phantoms and (what is about the same thing) to prevent nightmares.

Coral

A calcium mineral deposited by a species of marine animal. The precious variety is red (hardness about 3), the agatized variety is translucent brown and white. Precious coral is still in great demand in parts of southern Europe as a protection against the evil eye. It is also supposed to stop bleeding, cure madness, impart wisdom and ensure safe crossing over bodies of water.

Garnet

One of a series of aluminum silicates with magnesium, iron or manganese; or calcium silicates with chromium, aluminum and iron. Hardness 6 to 7.5. Colors may be red, green, yellow or brown, translucent or opaque. Those most often tumbled are translucent red (almandine). Like many red stones, garnets, because of their red color, were thought to convey immunity to wounds. By reversing the logic, the Hanzas, when fighting the British in northern India in the 1890s, used garnets as bullets in the belief that they would inflict an incurable wound.

Gypsum

Hydrated calcium sulfate. Hardness 2.5. The gem varieties are alabaster and satin spar. Stones of satin spar, yellowish in color, may show bands changing with the angle of observation, like cat's eye or tiger eye. No particular virtue is associated with this stone, except general good luck and lack of misfortune.

Hematite

Red oxide of iron. Hardness varies from 1 to 6.5. The harder varieties may be cut or tumble polished. Sacred to the god of war, the stone was believed to confer invulnerability. American Indians used the softer varieties of the stone (sometimes found in small geodes called Devil's Paint Pots, on eastern beaches) as war paint, and the hard stone in jewelry and as amulets, sometimes combined with turquoise. The hard stone appears dead black or silvery, but, if rubbed across a rough white surface, will leave a red streak.

Jade

A magnesium or aluminum silicate. The variety usually tumbled is jadeite, the sodium aluminum silicate, with a hardness of 7. Jade is the Chinese good luck stone par excellence, although other cultures have used it for ornamentation and amulets. The particular virtue of a piece of jade to the Chinese depends upon the way it is carved, but its primary influence is upon love. Indeed, the stone was known as "concentrated essence of love." Imperial or Kingfisher jade, of a transparent emerald green, is a very valuable gemstone.

Jasper

A microcrystalline quartz, but without the banding or translucency of agate or chalcedony. Hardness 7. It occurs, like agate, in a variety of colors. The green type was valuable for bringing rain (through an animistic association with green fields, probably), while other types were thought to occur in the head of a certain type of adder and hence were used to draw out venom. Like bloodstone, it was also thought to stop bleeding.

Jet

A compact form of coal used for jewelry. Sometimes black onyx is referred to as jet. Because of its softness it is easy to work and was often carved into talismanic figures by prehistoric man, or drilled to make beads used in bracelets and necklaces.

Lapis-Lazuli

A dark-blue sodium aluminum silicate, with sulfur, related to the popular tumbling material sodalite, but finer grained and darker in color; often contains "gold" flecks of iron pyrite. Hardness 5 to 5.5. A very popular stone with the ancients, who often referred to it as a sapphire. It was believed to be a cure for melancholy and for certain fevers (probably malaria).

Malachite

An intense green carbonate of copper, often with banding, in massive material, of lighter green. Hardness 3.5 to 4. The stone was used to drive away evil spirits, especially from the cradles of sleeping children. It could be made even more effective in this respect by a carving upon it the image of the sun.

Moonstone

Albite or sanidine feldspar that reflects a bluish sheen from certain crystal directions. The characteristic is known as adularescence. A potassium aluminum silicate, hardness 6. Supposed to arouse love; to determine the future of a love affair, the stone is placed in the mouth during a full moon. The medieval treatise that suggests this does not say in what form the good or bad tidings arrive. Perhaps the stone develops a bitter taste if things are not going well?

Onyx

A black form of calcite, hardness 3, sometimes with white bands. A good antidote to moonstone, as any onyx worn around the neck is supposed to alleviate the pangs of love and provoke discord.

Opal

An amorphous silicon dioxide, with water up to 10%, hardness 5 to 6. Precious opal (with lots of "fire") is usually too valuable for tumbler polishing. The colorless variety, hyalite, and fire opal (orange red and translucent), are often tumble polished. The opal, until relatively recent times, was the premier good luck stone. When it became more popular, with the major Australian finds, jewelers found themselves setting more and larger stones. Since opal cracks very easily when being set, they also found themselves cursing their bad luck in breaking valuable pieces, and the bad reputation spread until people began to think that the opal was bad luck for anyone who did not wear it as his or her birthstone (October in one modern system). We have not included birthstones among the superstitions described here because there are so many systems that it is safe to say that almost any stone a person likes has been conceived as his birthstone at some period in history.

Peridot, Olivine, "Crysolite"

A magnesium or iron silicate, hardness 6.5 to 7. The gem material is a translucent olive green. Said to dispel nightmares and, if strung on the hair of an ass and attached to the left arm, protect against evil spirits. Like the green malachite, it was also associated with the sun.

Pyrite or Fool's Gold

Iron sulphide, hardness 6 to 6.5. Like the clear quartz Herkimer diamonds, glittering yellow pyrite crystals were often carried in an American Indian's medicine bag as talismans.

Rock Crystal

Clear quartz, hardness 7. Herkimer diamonds (clear, perfectly faceted quartz crystals from Herkimer County, New York) and Cape May diamonds (clear, water-worn quartz pebbles from Cape May County, New Jersey) are good examples of this material, thought among early Christians to symbolize purity of soul. Cape May diamonds are tumbled, but most of the tumbling material, like that used by the Chinese to carve their crystal balls, is massive.

Ruby

A red form of corundum (aluminum oxide) colored by chromium oxide. Hardness 9. A precious stone believed to convey all sorts of virtues. Here are a few: remove evil thoughts; preserve health; control desire; dissipate pestilential vapors; reconcile disputes; guard possessions and confer invulnerability. To confer all except the latter, wearing the stone in jewelry on the left side of the body is sufficient. To become invulnerable, one must actually insert the ruby in the flesh. Ruby was one of the first precious stones to be made synthetically (in the 1890s). Inferior stones are often tumbled.

Sapphire

Blue corundum. Hardness 9. The best varieties are a very deep translucent blue. "Star" sapphires are more opaque and contain microscopic inclusions that produce the asterism or star effect. This stone was once very popular with sorcerers, since it enabled them to understand oracles and cast spells. It then became the most popular stone for ecclesiastical jewelry. It is also supposed to be an antidote to poison. The star variety is said to bring good luck and to ward off the evil eye.

Commonly Tumbled Stones: Characteristics and Folklore

Serpentine

A hydrated variety of magnesium silicate. Hardness varies widely, from 2 to 5. It also has a wide range of characteristics. Crysotile serpentine is a form of asbestos, while light translucent green Williamsite is a gemstone. The massive, mottled green ophiolite (snakestone) is thought (you guessed it) to draw out venom from snakebite. This is the variety most commonly tumbled.

Tiger Eye or Cat's Eye

Hard form of asbestos, usually from Africa, which shows bands of brown and yellow that change position with the angle of observation.

Topaz

Aluminum fluorosilicate; hardness 8. Not to be confused with the smoky quartz often sold in jewelry stores as "smoky topaz." True topaz comes in a variety of colors, from blue green to yellowish brown.

Turquoise

Hydrated basic aluminum phosphate with copper. Hardness 5 to 6. Ranges in color from sky blue with brown veins (the most precious type, from Iran) to brilliant blue-green. For some reason this stone is closely connected with horses and is supposed to prevent injury due to falls from horseback. The stone was sacred not only to the ancient Persians but also to many tribes of western Indians.

Glossary

Abrasives—Compounds such as silicon carbide that provide the grinding action in the tumbler as the stones move against each other. The size of the abrasive grains determines the amount of grinding action. Coarse grains remove large quantities of material; fine prepolish abrasives smooth out fine scratches and other surface defects.

Additives—Anything added to the basic tumbler charge of stones, water and abrasives: baking soda to prevent gas formation, soap to insure good surface wetting or buffering compounds to reduce impact between stones.

Balanced load—A tumbler charge in which the stone sizes have been selected to give an optimum mixture of small, medium and large-sized pieces, providing ideal tumbling action.

Baroque—An irregularly shaped gemstone or pearl.

Blistering—Surface fracturing that may occur in transparent stones such as amethyst, in which a small section is separated by cracking from the parent material without being completely detached.

Buffering agents—Materials such as plastic pellets or wood chips that cushion the impact of stones against each other in the tumbler.

Burnishing—A term from metalworking, in which a surface is polished by smoothing down irregularities without removing material. A nonabrasive polishing method.

Capillary action—The rise of liquid in narrow tubes through molecular processes. May be responsible for tumbler barrel leakage in some cases.

Charging—Loading the barrel with the materials necessary for tumbling.

Cleavage plane—A "fault line" in a stone along which it is most likely to break; used especially of materials such as feldspar which tend to break into planar tablets or cubes.

Conchoidal fracture—A type of stone fracture in which the broken surfaces are curved like the surface of a shell. Characteristic of hard, fine-grained materials such as agate.

Diamond saw—Not a saw at all, but a very fast-cutting grinding wheel made by impregnating a metal disc with diamond particles.

Electrodeposition—A type of electroplating in which a very heavy coat of metal, which may include metal crystals, is deposited on an object by electrolysis.

Electroforming—The production of metal articles by deposition of a metal upon an electrode.

Embedding—The inclusion of particles of a foreign material in a rock matrix, such as the characteristic iron pyrite specks in lapis lazuli. Also the mounting of a gemstone in a surrounding of metal, for example by electrodeposition.

Epoxy compounds—Synthetic resins used as adhesives and fillers in jewelry making. Most consist of two parts: the resin itself, which remains liquid until activated and cured by the second component, the hardener.

Even load—As distinguished from a balanced load, a tumbler charge consisting, usually, of all large stones to provide a less irregular shape to the finished gemstones.

Faceting—Cutting of stone surfaces, usually with a diamond abrasive, to provide a series of tiny planes or facets that reflect light and increase the brilliance of the stone.

Gemstones—Strictly speaking, any pieces of mineral used for personal adornment. Gemstones are generally divided into precious and semiprecious categories. Precious stones, such as rubies, emeralds or diamonds, are sold by the carat; semiprecious stones, such as agate or obsidian, by the piece or by the ounce. There is no hard and fast dividing line; amethyst was once a precious stone until major new discoveries made it semiprecious; some turquoise is sold by the carat, other grades by the pound, and so on for all stones.

Geodes—Mineral concretions formed by deposits from solution in natural cavities, generally volcanic "bubbles." Geodes are usually spherical, may be hollow and encrusted with crystals on the inner surface of the sphere, water-filled or solid.

Gloppies—Slang for free-form silver or gold nuggets made by half melting pieces of scrap so that they fuse together or by fully liquefying the metal and dropping it into ice water (*drop castings*).

Goldstone—A man-made stone consisting of glass containing millions of gold-colored metallic flakes. The stone is made in Italy by what is said to be a secret process.

Grinding wheel—For lapidary work, generally a corundum abrasive wheel with some provision for keeping the surface wet so that the stone being ground does not overheat or flake.

Grooving—Cutting a groove around the circumference of a stone with a grinding wheel or diamond saw to hold a wire mounting.

Inclusions—Pieces of a dissimilar mineral embedded in a stone matrix. See *Embedding*.

Indexing—A feature of certain diamond saws for cutting slabs or preforms, in which the blade moves laterally by a preset amount after each cut.

Intermediate grind—Step in tumbling after rough grind. Some material is removed from the stone during this process, but its primary purpose is to re-

Glossary

move scratches from the coarse abrasive and prepare the surface for the pre-polish step.

Jeweler's rouge—A type of fine polish; usually an oxide of tin or iron.

Jeweler's saw—A hand tool shaped like a jigsaw and designed to accept very fine wirelike blades for precise metal cutting.

Lost-wax casting—An ancient metal-casting technique recently revived for casting intricate objects. The hot metal when poured melts and replaces a wax model.

Matrix—Mass of rock enclosing crystals or gemstone; also used to mean rock surrounding inclusions.

Mineralogy—The science of minerals, dealing with formation, crystal structure, location and identification.

Notching—A series of shallow cuts in the edge of a baroque stone to accept claws or wires holding the stone in a setting.

Oscillation—Movement back and forth. Method of creating motion of the charge in a vibratory tumbler, as distinguished from rotation in standard tumblers.

Pellet medium—Plastic pellets added to the tumbling charge to serve as a buffering agent and prevent too-violent collision of the stones. May also refer to dry tumbling abrasives that can be used in vibratory tumblers, in which the abrasive and a carrier are combined in granular form.

Pickling solution—Acid or basic solution used to clean metals of flux and oxidation after hot working or soldering.

Pitting—Defects in tumbling material. Voids or soft places in the mineral matrix that will not polish and which accumulate abrasives from previous steps.

Polish—Any of a class of extremely fine abrasives, such as tin oxide, that impart a lustrous finish to stones as the final step in tumbling.

Preforms—Shapes such as hearts or crosses cut on a diamond saw prior to tumble polishing.

Prepolish—The last abrasive step prior to polishing. Removes fine scratches and provides a matte surface.

Primary fracture—A flaw that extends from side to side of the stone and will eventually cause it to break.

Refractive index—A measure of the amount that a light ray is bent when travelling from air into another substance. The brilliance of a diamond is caused by its high refractive index. When making repairs on stones, transparent epoxy, if it has approximately the same refractive index as the stone, will be almost invisible.

Rotary tumbler—The most widely used type of rock tumbler. A charge of minerals and abrasives in water is contained inside a rotating, generally horizontal barrel. The rotation of the barrel causes the stones to "tumble" over one another and the abrasive trapped between the stones grinds the surfaces.

Rough—A mineral, broken or unbroken, prior to the first stage of tumbling.

Rough grind—The first stage in tumbling, when a coarse abrasive is used to smooth and round the surfaces of the freshly broken material.

Sheet metal settings—Jewelry findings cut from sheet metal such as silver. Prongs to hold baroques or cut stones are also cut from the sheet to form an integral part of the setting.

Silicon carbide—A very hard abrasive made by heating silica—silicon dioxide or quartz is the major constituent of sand—in the presence of carbon.

Slab—Thin plane section of stone which may be tumble polished on both sides.

Slabbing—Cutting slabs or slices of stone from a larger piece with a diamond saw.

Slurry—The viscous solution of water, abrasives, rock dust and additives in which the stones inside the tumbler are immersed. The consistency of the slurry is very important to successful rock tumbling.

Spalling—Pitting or flaking of a stone surface, as distinguished from chipping that occurs at thin edges. Spalling is evidence of abrasive action too severe for the general structural integrity of the stone.

Steel tumbling shot—Highly polished steel shapes, such as ball bearings, used in a tumbler to clean and burnish metals.

Tumbling—The process of grinding and polishing by rotating or vibrating a mass of stones in a progressively finer series of abrasive solutions.

Tumbling tablets—Proprietary products that, when added to the water in a tumbler, increase its viscosity. Their action is similar to that of buffering agents or sugar.

Up-eye—A small bell-shaped cap fixed to a baroque stone with epoxy and containing a ring that may be used to join the stone to a setting, as for earrings, or to join stones together in bracelets or necklaces.

Vibratory tumblers—Rock tumblers in which the barrel containing the stones vibrates rapidly, rather than rotates, to tumble the stones inside.

Viscosity—The tendency of a fluid to resist relative motion within itself. Syrup is more viscous than water. Tumbling solutions should have enough viscosity (increased by adding sugar) to prevent violent collisions of the stones in the batch.

Water glass—A solution of sodium silicate that dries to a hard transparent finish.

Wire wrapping—Method of securing baroque stones in jewelry by wrapping them in ductile silver, copper, bronze or gold wire.

Sources of Supply

In addition to the individuals and companies listed in the acknowledgments, the authors have found the following generally superior sources of rough, tumbling supplies and lapidary books. Many other excellent suppliers can be found in the directory published by *The Lapidary Journal* as part of its annual issue.

COLLECTING GUIDES

Gems and Minerals
  P.O. Box 687
  Mentone, CA 92359
The Lapidary Journal
  P.O. Box 80937
  3564 Kettner Blvd.
  San Diego, CA 92138

EQUIPMENT

Lapidabrade, Inc.
  8 E. Eagle Rd.
  Havertown, PA 19083

FINDINGS

Crestmark Manufacturing Co.
  17-25 Camden Street
  Paterson, NJ 07503

Gems 'N' Silver by Sassen, Inc.
  12 Castle St.
  Great Barrington, MA 01230
The Sandvigs
  902 N. Riverside Ave.
  Medford, OR 97501

GENERAL SUPPLIES

Buried Treasure, Inc.
  12124 Nebel St.
  Rockville, MD 20852
Dinosaur Gift and Mineral Shop
  Route 6
  Brewster, NY 10519
Frazier's Gems and Minerals
  115 Center St., Box 177
  Seville, OH 44273
Gilman's
  Hellertown, PA 18055

Heike's
    208-2nd North St.
    Wenona, IL 61377
Zymex
    900 West Los Vellecitos Blvd.
    San Marcos, CA 92069

ROUGH

Arrow Gems and Minerals
    9827 Cave Creek Rd.
    Phoenix, AR 85020
Aztec Gem and Mineral Supply
    P.O. Box 15272
    2531 E. Madison
    Phoenix, AR 85060
Booth's Lapidary Supply
    Lane City Road
    Boling, TX 77420
Dawn Mining and Minerals
    Box 105
    Florissant, CO 80816
Deming Enterprises
    Route 1, Box 202
    Deming, NM 88030
Ramco Specialties, Inc.
    220 S. 13th St.
    Allentown, PA 18102
The Treasure Chest
    P.O. Box 54, Rt. 40
    Havre de Grace, MD 21078

Index

Abrasive materials, 32, 62, 64, 65, 73
  amounts, 71
    in intermediate/fine grind, 78t
    in prepolish cycle, 84t
    in rough grind, 64t, 66
  breakdown of, 51–52
  compounds, dry, 49
  solution viscosity, 50–54, 67, 68, 72, 92. *See also* Slurry
Additives, 4, 34, 94
  amounts, 76
    in intermediate/fine grind, 78t
    in polish cycle, 88t
    in prepolish cycle, 84t
    in rough grind, 64t
  types, 4, 34, 94
Agate, 7, 63t
  banded, 17
  Botswana, 54
  Brazilian, 97
  eye, 17
  lace, 17, 20, 89
  Maguey, 17
  moss, 68, 89
  Sagonite, 89
Agatized coral, 96
Amazonite, 63t, 83
Amethyst, 60, 73, 118
  price, 20
  tumbling group, 63t

Antifreeze, use in tumbling, 31
Apache Tears, 53, 57, 58, 62, 70, 109, 112
  as carrier, 97, 98, 100
  tumbling group, 63t
Attack, 115

Bacterial action, 94
Baking soda, 34, 66, 78t, 83, 84t, 93. *See also* Additives
Balanced load, 53, 59, 62, 66, 92. *See also* Tumblers
Baroques, 2, 112–130
Barrel, 36, 37. *See also* Tumblers
  effective diameter, and operating speed, 40t
  effects of shape, 90
  speed, 90
  stops, 98
Beach pebbles, 1, 21, 27, 57, 70
Bearings, in tumbler construction, 26. *See also* Tumblers
Beeswax for stone setting, 114
Beggar beads, 125
Bell caps, 118
Beryl, 8
Blistering of stones, 65, 107. *See also* Defective polished stones
Bow drill, 2. *See also* Tools
Bracelets, 122
Breakage, 104

Buffering agents, 33, 66, 73, 80, 83, 91
Buffing, 83
Burnishing, 87, 89

Cabochons, 49, 95
Cages, jewelry, 134, 136, 146
Cape May diamonds, 1
Carnelian, 57, 63t, 69
Castings, 148
Cedar chips, as additives, 94
Center polish, 106. *See also* Defective polished stones
Chemical action, 93
Claw settings, 139
Cleanness, 18. *See also* Rough, characteristics for tumbling
Collecting rocks
  guides and maps, 8
  safety, 13
  sources, 9–13
  tools, 11
Color, 17. *See also* Rough, characteristics for tumbling
Compatible tumbling materials, 62, 63t
Crystal balls, 2
Cullet (glass), 60, 89

Defective polished stones
  blistering, 107
  breakage, 104
  centers only polished, 106
  edges only polished, 106
  flats, 106
  incomplete polish, 106
  no polish, 104
  scratches, 108
  spalling, 106
  veins, 108
Diamond saws, 153
  coolants, 154–155
  slab saws, 156
  trim saws, 153
Display racks, 127
Drilling, 162
  machines, 162–163, 164–165
  procedures, 162
Drive belt size, 43–45
Drive shafts, 37, 38
  diameters, 45
  spacing, 44
  speed, 41, 42, 43
Drop castings (gloppies), 148

Earrings, 127
Edge polish, 106. *See also* Defective polished stones
Effective barrel diameter, 40, 41. *See also* Barrels
Electrodeposition, 148
Epidote, 118
Epoxy, 89, 109, 112, 114
  application of, 114–115, 118–119
  setting time, 117
Even load, 92. *See also* Tumblers, loading

Feldspar, 32, 61, 108
Field trips, 9. *See also* Collecting rocks
Findings (jewelry), 114, 117–118
Flat stones, 106. *See also* Defective polished stones
Fractures
  brittle, 15
  on cleavage planes, 15
  conchoidal, 15

Garnet, 63t, 118
Gas buildup, 93, 94
Gem trees, 127
Geodes
  rind, 17
  tumbling in slabs, 100
Glass. *See* Cullet
Goldstone, 60, 63t
Grain, 16. *See also* Rough, characteristics for tumbling
Grinding wheel, 160, 162
Grooving. *See* Notching

Hammers, 31. *See also* Tools
Hardness, 14. *See also* Rough, characteristics for tumbling
Hexagonal barrels, 90

Inclusions, 17
Indexing saw, 160. *See also* Diamond saws
Inspection of stones, 76. *See also* Rough, characteristics for tumbling

Jasper, 17, 21
Jump rings, 119

Lapidary Journal, 9, 20, 30
Lucite embedding, 129, 130

Malachite, 16, 17, 63t
Material, purchased, 20. *See also* Rough, characteristics for tumbling

Index

Medieval jewelry, 3
Metal polishing, 16
Methyl methacrylate, 114
Mineral oil, 109
Mineral veins, 10
Mineralogical societies, 9. *See also* Collecting rocks
Moebius strip, 134

Necklaces, 125
Notching and grooving of baroques, 158

Obsidian, 54, 55, 60, 65, 89, 118
Onyx, 118
Operating speeds of tumbler motors, 40. *See also* Tumblers
Opticon, 109

Panning, 80
Pendants, 125, 126
Petrified wood, 7
Pins, 127
Pitting, 16, 17. *See also* Defective polished stones
Polish, lack of, 104, 106. *See also* Defective polished stones
Polish
    amounts, 88t
    recommended for tumbling, 106
Power supply to workshop, 31
Preforms
    cutting, 160
        on indexing saw, 160
        manually, 160
    tumbling, 26, 49, 95–96
Prepolish, 76, 80, 83, 84t
Prong settings for rings, 146, 158
Pulley (sheave) diameters, 42
Pulleys, 42. *See also* Tumblers, construction
Pyrite, 17

Quarries, 13

Red veining, 108
Rings, 119, 120, 122
Road cuts, 11
Rock-breaking tools, 31, 57. *See also* specific tools
Rock shops, 9
Rockhounds. *See* Collecting rocks
Rocks and Minerals, 9

Rose quartz, 32, 60
Rough, characteristics for tumbling, 16–18, 20. *See also* specific traits
Rutilated quartz, 89

Saw ends, 101
Scratch marks, 108
Sheaves, 37. *See also* Tumblers, construction
Sheet metal settings, 138, 140
Silicon carbide, 2, 3, 52
Silver annealing, 132
Slab saw, 156, 157. *See also* Diamond saws
Slabbing small stones, 157, 158
Slabs, 95–100
Slurry, 93. *See also* Abrasives; Additives
Snowflake obsidian, 17
Soap, as additive, 72, 73, 83, 87. *See also* Additives
Sodalite, 17
Soldered settings, 141–145
Sorting stones, 72
Spalling, 49, 55, 58, 76, 83, 87, 106. *See also* Defective polished stones
Speed control of tumbler motors, 30, 36, 92
Sterling silver
    in jewelry, 131
    wire cross-sections, 133, 134
Stone carving, 2
Stone repair, 109
Stone sorting, 69, 123
Storage of rough, 32
Stream beds, for prospecting, 11
Structural integrity, 15. *See also* Rough characteristics for tumbling
Sugar, as additive, 73, 78, 82, 83, 87. *See also* Additives
Surface inspection, 17

Tension mounts, 138
Thickeners. *See* Additives
Time in tumbler, 51, 52
    in intermediate/fine grind, 78t
    in polish cycle, 88t
    in prepolish cycle, 84t
    in rough grind, 64t
Tin oxide, 87, 89
Titanium oxide, 89
Tourmaline, 8, 63t
Trim saw, 153. *See also* Diamond saws
Tripoli, 32
Tumble-polishing metal, 149–153
Tumblers
    barrel seals, 23

Tumblers, cont'd.
  barrel stops, 29
  barrels, 22, 23, 25, 26
  capacity, 25, 26, 30
  charging, 50, 66. *See also* Abrasives;
    Additives
  construction, 35, 36, 37
  design calculations, 39, 40, 41
  drives, 23, 24, 25, 26, 27, 30
  hexagonal, 27
  industrial, 3, 4
  home-made, 4, 30
  motor, 30
  motor temperature, 24
  mounting, 32
  noise, 55, 92, 93
  power consumption, 22, 30
  price, 22, 25, 26, 49, 50
  single-shaft, 28, 29
  size, 27
  small, 22
  vibrating, 46, 49, 56

Tumbletrol, 73, 82, 83, 87
Tumbling action, 91
Tumbling, as a hobby, 4
Tumbling materials, 7. *See also* Abrasives;
    Additives; Rough
Tumbling shot, 149
Turquoise, 16, 110, 118
Twisted wire, 134

Uniform (even) load, 59, 60
Up eyes, 112

Vibratory drives, 46, 48
Viscosity, solution, 33, 91, 92. *See also*
    Abrasives

Waste disposal, 31
Water glass, 110
Wire wrapping techniques, 131–133
Workshop requirements, 31

Zodiac signs, 127

Christopher Hyde, who received his MA from the University of Rochester, has written articles for numerous technical, trade and national magazines, including *Saturday Review, Argosy* and *Philadelphia Magazine*. His many interests include mineral and rock collecting and silversmithing. Hyde has worked in public relations for many years and is presently the Director of Public Relations at Weightman, Inc., in Philadelphia. Mr. Hyde is the author of *A Week Down in Devon* (Chilton).

Richard A. Matthews is a mechanical engineer who started rock collecting as a hobby many years ago. As his interest grew into rock tumbling and other related lapidary areas, Matthews opened his own lapidary shop in Allentown, Pennsylvania, where today he is constantly busy working his wide variety of tumbling machines.